I Heard
Heaven
Proclaim

D0068116

Bill Yount
foreword by Jane Hansen

Published by:

McDougal Publishing
P.O. Box 3595
Hagerstown, MD 21742-3595
www.mcdougalpublishing.com

McDougal Publishing is a ministry of The McDougal Foundation, Inc., a Maryland nonprofit corporation dedicated to the
spreading of the Gospel of the Lord Jesus Christ to as many
people as possible in the shortest time possible.

All Scripture references are taken from the Authorized King
James Version of the Bible unless otherwise noted. Scripture
references marked NIV are taken from the New International
Version of the Bible, copyright © 1973, 1978, 1984 by International Bible Society, Colorado Springs, Colorado.

ISBN 1-58158-075-4

Printed in the United States of America
For Worldwide Distribution

DEDICATION

I dedicate this book to my beloved, beautiful wife, Dagmar, who is "the wind beneath my wings." Thank you for bearing with me the many nights the Lord would awaken me and speak to me, disrupting your rest as I crawled out of bed. You are my most powerful intercessor, my best friend and lover.

Thank you, Naomi, Danielle and Joel, for teaching me so much more than I could teach you. You give me reasons to pray and rejoice as I watch you all grow into the likeness of Jesus Christ. "There's no greater joy than to know my children walk in truth!"

I dedicate this to the best mother on earth—mine. Thanks, Mom, for taking us children to church when we didn't want to go.

I dedicate this book to my Dad, who has gone on ahead of us to be with Jesus. I know you are watching from Heaven's grandstands, cheering the rest of our family homeward.

I dedicate this book to one of my many spiritual mothers, Jackie Fields, whose home has been a resting place in God's presence. It's home away from home for my wife and me.

I also dedicate this book to Luella Bracken, who has

gone to be with Jesus at the time of this writing. She was a special spiritual mother to me and her prayers have greatly influenced my life and family.

I love you all, and I thank Jesus Christ, who has gone to prepare a place for us to live together forever.

ACKNOWLEDGMENTS

I want to thank Jane Hansen, the president of Aglow International, for opening the door so wide for me when all other doors seemed closed. The Aglow sisters around the world have been powerful intercessors for me and my family as well as for my ministry. The Aglow ministry became a platform where I could grow in my gifting in an atmosphere of love and acceptance. You will always be in my heart. I would not have made it without you all. You are touching the lives of more men than you realize. God bless every Aglow sister on earth!

Thank you, Mildred Weller, for all the times you were there to answer the phone when I didn't know where to turn. You are ninety years old now at the time of this writing and have more wisdom for me each day! God always answers my questions through you. May the Lord greatly use your book, *The Spirit Within*. Please live forever—I will always need your divine counsel.

Thank you, Rev. Ben Murray, executive director of Road to New Life Ministries, for mentoring me for many years.

Thank you, Rev. Lynn Singleton, executive director, Dr. Clay Norton and all the Mount Hope Prison

Ministry family, for twenty-three years of teaching me by example that to be a servant is the highest calling of God.

Thank you, Dr. Terry King, for believing in me when I couldn't believe in myself.

Thank you, Pastor Brian Flook, for motivating me further than I thought possible to go.

Thank you, Rabbi Ted Simon, for letting me take your place to carry your shofar down the aisle for the Young Messiah Celebration. That celebration turned into a full-time ministry for me blowing the shofar across this nation and into other parts of the world.

Thank you, Rev. Don Kretzer, for blowing the shofar with me to awaken the Body of Christ to her Jewish roots, to stand for Israel.

Thank you, Rev. Al Thomas, for sharing the ups and downs of full-time ministry. I pray your powerful book *I Saw the Lord* touches many people as you have touched my life.

Thank you, Rev. James Horst, for encouraging me so often and traveling with me at times.

Thank you, Brother Antoine Rajahpillay, for helping to pray me out of the emergency room on March 10, 2003. I know you have a great gift of healing in your hands.

Thank you, Steve Shultz of The Elijah List, for opening the door for many of my words to go worldwide and encouraging me in so many ways.

Thank you, Bishop Frank Costantino, for prophesying over me, "The words that you speak will be greater than who you are!"

Thank you, Dr. Gertrude Dixon, for your many

prophecies over my life and family that are coming to pass more each day.

Thank you, Carol Miller and Margaret Heiser, for all the glory meetings and encouragement.

Thank you, Mary Rodger, for your generous hospitality to my family.

Thank you, Joey Stratton, for, in spite of afflictions, lifting us continually before the Father.

A special thank you, Pat Myers, for the hours of hard work you spent to make me sound better than I write.

And thanks to so many who have blessed me and my family and touched our lives....

Thank you all,

Bill, Dagmar, Naomi, Danielle and Joel Yount

"Bill Yount's book *I Heard Heaven Proclaim* will rock your world and capture your heart at the same time. You will hear and see part of our Master's plans for the days we live in. With elation, I highly recommend the meditation and revelation contained in these pages."

— Jim Goll
Ministry to the Nations
Author of *The Coming Prophetic Revolution*

"Bill Yount has a wonderful way of relating truth and getting revelation from God through ordinary situations which you or I would pass by. Along with his prophetic words and insights, he still has that delightful childlike amazement at the goodness of God. That's something that God loves. We should never lose that capacity to enjoy our "heavenly Daddy " and His awesome care for us. Bill's stories and words remind me that it is all about relationship and not "ministry."

— Kathie Walters
Good News Ministries
Author of *Living in the Supernatural*

"I have known Bill Yount for many years. Many know Bill as a prophet. I know him as a friend. He is a quiet man of integrity, trust and humility, and he possesses another rare quality: he hears from Heaven, but keeps his feet on the earth. We have ministered together many times in churches and conferences. Over the years, as his ministry has grown and his influence has increased, he has remained the same. May this be true of all of God's servants."

— Al Thomas
Celebrating His Life Ministries
Author of *I Saw the Lord*

CONTENTS

FOREWORD

My association with Bill Yount goes back several years and has come through the Aglow ministry. We have been blessed by Bill's prophetic ministry at a number of our Aglow conferences. I have also been personally encouraged by prophetic words he has shared with me over the years.

There are many prophetic voices in the Body of Christ today, each with their own distinctive style of expression. Bill Yount's prophetic gift is unique in that he often paints a picture of the word in a way that strikes a chord in your heart.

Through the events of everyday life, God gives Bill profound insights which he then communicates in such a clear and down-to-earth way. You might say that Bill's style for the prophetic word is like *The Message* is to the written Word—it is a God-given impartation in words and images that are easy to relate to. At the same time, Bill's depth of insight results in many an "aha!" moment. There are also words in this book that are powerful and passionate and so resonate with the voice of the Lord that your spirit leaps in response.

Wherever you are in your spiritual journey with the Lord, you will find words in this book to encourage you along the way. You may be at the beginning of your walk, having just met Jesus, the path stretching endlessly before you. Perhaps you've run the race and are nearing the finish line, with Heaven seeming closer than ever before. Or maybe you are somewhere in between, just putting one foot in front of the other, trusting Him every step of the way because the path before you seems clouded. Whether you are in the midst of a "mountaintop" experience, or in the "valley of the shadow of death," the prophetic words contained in this volume will bring strength, hope, joy and confirmation of those things the Lord is doing in your life.

You will also get a glimpse of the purposes of God for His people Israel, for the Body of Christ and for those yet to come into His Kingdom. You will find this book expresses the heart of God on both a personal level for every believer and from a broader perspective on a corporate level for the Body of Christ.

I know your walk with the Lord will be enriched by the messages that are found within the pages of this book.

Jane Hansen
President, Aglow International
Edmonds, Washington

INTRODUCTION

Four years ago I finished writing a book similar to this one. Upon finishing the book and feeling excited about getting it published, I heard the voice of the Lord say, "Take this book and bury it in the backyard in your garden!" Perhaps it meant so much to me that I needed to die to the thought of ever having my book published.

I took the manuscript (a copy of it) and in the middle of winter digging into the frozen ground I buried it in the backyard in our garden. I didn't have the level of faith to bury the original copy itself. The next spring when we had our garden rototilled, I noticed the manuscript was not found. I must have buried it deep enough.

As I buried it, I sensed the Lord saying, "Whatever you plant in a garden will grow!" I then realized that Jesus Himself was planted in a garden tomb and that He was raised from the dead in a garden. And just like whatever is planted in a garden, when it grows, it will appear different from the original seed that was buried...especially when it gets watered by tears, is crushed through brokenness and then dies a thousand deaths. And so it is with this book that has finally surfaced and broken through the crust of the earth—this earthen vessel. This book is different from the one I planted. And I also arn not the same man I was four years ago. But I believe this is the book the Lord intended to harvest at this time.

Many of the prophetic words and the ministry the Lord has given me come out of my everyday life with my family. My children have given me my best sermons and prophetic teachings. I preach to myself as well as to other ministers: "If we would stay home more, we would pray more. Our families will drive us to our knees!"

It seems that in our most difficult moments, Heaven speaks to us and descends a little closer to earth. Often life apart from a heavenly perspective doesn't make sense. Many times I have said to the Lord, "Lord, this isn't making any sense down here." In those dark moments, I've heard Heaven proclaim: "It does from up here!"

A stanza of a poem entitled "My Masterpiece," by Robert Service:

"A humdrum way I go to-night,
From all I hoped and dreamed remote:
Too late…a better man must write
That Little Book I Never Wrote."

PART ONE

IN EVERYDAY LIFE

One

Healing Runs in My Family

When I was five years old, my mother used to embarrass me in front of the hometown folks (my hometown being Ford City, Pennsylvania, where I lived until my late twenties). Mom would seemingly wait until she got me around a whole lot of people and then she would tell everybody, "This is my little preacher! This is my little missionary!" I have now been a home missionary through our church for the past thirty years and I preach a little.

The prophetic word my mother spoke over me was to be tested two years later. Five of us kids on one bicycle were flying down a steep hill. (We could have been charged with bicycle abuse today.) I was the smallest of the five, so I was sitting in the basket up front. We lost our balance after losing the brakes and we went sailing through the air, but not with the greatest of ease. We crashed headlong onto the dirt road. I suffered the worst damage, hitting my head hard as I landed.

A year later, the doctor discovered a bone growth

rapidly developing on my head from the injury. As they were taking x-rays, they also found a brain tumor. They would need to operate to take out the tumor and then chip away the bone growth.

The doctor sent me to a specialist at Mercy Hospital in Pittsburgh, Pennsylvania. It was a Catholic hospital, and Mom had all the nuns praying for me! I thank God for those nuns. The morning came for the operation to take the brain tumor out. For some reason, I noticed Mom looked happy coming into my room. She said, "Bill, they just took another set of x-rays to know how to take the tumor out, but they can't find it! It's not there now!"

The Lord later showed me the power of my mother's words spoken over me two years earlier. When the brain tumor showed up in me, it was the words my mother spoke over me that ate the tumor! She had the mind of God for my life, so it was the Lord Himself speaking my destiny through her! Therefore, heaven and earth would have to pass away first before her spoken prophetic word would pass away. The doctors still had to operate to chip away the bone growth on my head. It was a serious operation, but the prophetic word brought me through the valley of the shadow of death…and this wouldn't be the last time.

Just recently, on March 10, 2003, at the age of fifty-four, I experienced a heart attack. I believe now that once again I am being "attacked by healing"!

The Lord has shown me personally that one of the reasons I am still here is because healing runs in my family. It started on my mother's side. When she was only twelve years old, she saw her mother (who lived to be ninety-four), healed instantly of a huge goiter that disappeared from my grandmother's neck in a Kathryn Kuhlman meeting. The next second she heard a little boy beside her scream out…"Mommy, where are you?" The boy's eyes were opened for the very first time in his life! Faith comes by hearing, but when you see miracles, you not only believe in them—you live by them.

My mother had cancer thirty years ago, but God has healed her of it. She has had many afflictions in her body, but God keeps touching and healing her. She had bypass surgery in her early seventies, but she just keeps going strong. She is almost eighty now at the time of this writing, and she works part-time midnight shift (12-8 AM) in a rest home taking care of older people. I believe it all started when my mother saw God healing my grandmother and that little boy.

My sister, Carol, who is also a believer, called me to pray for her recently. She said the doctor found a mass the size of a golf ball near her ovary. I reminded her that healing runs in our family. She and her husband held hands as my wife, Dagmar, and I prayed. The next morning my sister woke up at 4:00 o'clock and felt a warmth go over her from her waist down. She felt peace during her MRI test that morning. She called the next day after getting the MRI report back— nothing was there! The nurse even reexamined her, but it wasn't there now. The doctor told her, "You just got a miracle!" My sister is telling everyone that God healed her. She can't sleep at night because she is so excited. She said that this has awakened her and her husband and that she is going to praise the Lord every day of her life.

I sense God is up to releasing a healing momentum this hour for healing to run in our families so the generations to come can say, "Healing runs in my family!" Healing started on my mother's side, and on my heavenly Father's side it runs through my veins. If you have a mother or father or grandparents who have been healed by the Lord, expect your healing to run right down through your family tree. I believe the Lord is releasing generational healings this hour because of Calvary's tree. Get ready to receive!

Two

I Know How Long God's Arm Is

Mom used to make us kids go to church. Dad didn't go for many years, but Mom would tell us, "As long as you're under our roof, you will be under the roof of God's house!" I used to thank God before I was even saved that our church had a balcony in it. It didn't seem to matter to my mother where we sat as long as we got under that roof. We would get the highest and farthest seat from the pulpit—the last row in the balcony. Up there we would talk, of course, and get away with a lot of things, or so we thought.

Then one Sunday morning a lady got up in the pulpit and began to sing "He Touched Me." I suddenly discovered how long God's arm is. It's as long as the pulpit is from the balcony, for He touched me at that moment through that song. I got up from my friends and came down the steps from the balcony and walked right down the center aisle to the altar. God is the only person I know who can interrupt His own service and not get upset. I gave my life to the Lord that morning, and I was never the same again.

I was nineteen years old at the time and began working in a steel mill near Pittsburgh. I worked there seven years, and little by little the Lord began speaking to me. One lunch break I was reading the Scriptures in Jeremiah 1:5: *"Before I formed thee in the belly I knew thee; and before thou camest forth out of the womb I sanctified thee, and I ordained thee a prophet unto the nations."* That scripture seemed to leap up off the page for me at that moment. But I thought, "How could this be? Here I am working in a dusty old steel mill." I knew then that the Lord had something more for me than just working there and making money to hopefully get married one day. But He quickly was making it clear to me that His calling would soon take me out of that factory to follow Him.

Even when I knew that He clearly had told me to "lay down my nets" and leave the factory, I still dragged my feet. Finally, about a year later while I was on my lunch break one day, He got through to me. In the Spirit, I saw the Lord as though He was walking past the factory where I was eating my lunch alone and He pointed at me and said, "Son, I'm calling you for the very last time." I knew it was one of those now-or-never moments when I needed to step out now to follow or I might never know what I had missed if I would have stayed behind.

I gave two weeks' notice to resign from my job. Thirty days after I left the factory, that steel mill began to shut down and never reopened. I knew that God did not call me because I was so spiritual; He called me because He was looking out for me. He wanted to be my only security.

I was now twenty-seven years old and still living at

home. God stirred my nest to leave my parents by using my brother, Jim, who lived near Frederick, Maryland. I would visit him and his family at times, and when I would visit their church, I felt peace. God's peace was confirming His direction for me to leave my parents and move in with my brother and his family. I had saved a nice bank account for my dream of getting married one day, although I had no prospects at the time. When visiting churches and prayer meetings with my brother, it seemed I met the poorest Christians in the state of Maryland. Everywhere I went, everyone needed finances.

One night after leaving a prayer meeting and going home to my brother's basement where I had set up my little abode, I sensed the Lord wanted to do some serious talking with me. I sensed the Lord saying to me, "Bill, I want to talk to you about My money in your bank account, the money you are saving to get married with. Especially since I haven't given you the one to marry yet, you don't really need that money right now." I didn't want to hear that. In case the Lord did not know everything, I told Him how hard I had worked for seven years to save that money. But He seemed to stop communicating when I started to explain that to Him.

The next day at a prayer meeting, a businessman stood up and shared that he was in financial need of three thousand dollars or his business would go under in a week's time. When I got home to my brother's house, I figured I'd better give this man that amount before I heard of a more expensive need. I wrote the check out and gave it through the pastor, so to this day that man never knew where it came from.

After thirty short days, the Lord spoke again to me. I noticed when I would obey His voice, He would continue talking to me, but when I would hear and not obey, He seemed to become silent. That night in my brother's basement, the Lord spoke again: "Bill, I did not call you to leave your mother and father to cleave to your brother!" (It almost sounded scriptural.) "I am calling you alone to know Me and find in Me your identity and security. I am calling you to a life of faith to trust Me to provide for all your needs." I remember it like it was yesterday.

I loaded up everything I owned in my little Mustang car and started to drive out of my brother's driveway and on to Interstate 70. When God had called me from the factory, He had given me the verse about Abraham going out not knowing where he was going but he was following God's voice. All I knew was that the Lord had called me from the factory, from my parents' home and from my brother's house, and now I was going out not knowing where I was going.

I started driving down Interstate 70, and after a while I saw this exit sign for a place called Hagerstown, Maryland. At the time, I didn't know why I took that exit, but looking back I know now that God knows how to drive an automobile. When we don't know where we are going and have no agenda of our own, He can steer us easier as long as we are moving.

I drove into the city and parked the car in a lot and began to walk down an alley to get on the main street. As I cut through the alley, I came to a Christian coffeehouse. I walked in and they were having a Bible study on the life of Abraham…going out not knowing where he was going. I felt peace. I met a brother in the Lord there, Rev. Ben Murray, the founder of Mount Hope Prison Ministry. The ministry started in two little rooms inside that coffeehouse and today touches prisoners nationwide. I later would start going to the prisons with him and become full-time in the prison ministry for the next twenty-three years.

I had some money from my bank account left, and it seemed that a spirit of giving came over me and I joyfully would bless people in need. That had to be God, not me! I remember living at the YMCA in town and being about to run out of my money.

The next Sunday morning I attended a church called Faith Chapel. I had three dollars left and I felt the Lord saying to give it in the offering plate. You couldn't have food in your room at the YMCA, so I knew this meant no lunch. I gave it. Since I was new in town, no one knew me, but after the service a couple came up and introduced themselves and asked me a Heaven-sent question: "Would you like to come home with us and have lunch?" They never saw anyone so thrilled at being invited to their home to eat with them.

That evening, Rev. Terry King, the pastor of Faith Chapel at the time, was preaching. During his sermon the Lord stopped him with a word of knowledge. Brother Terry said, "There is someone here tonight who has stepped out to obey the Lord to follow Him. He has told you already that He is going to provide for you. But this is like putting the icing on the cake. God says He is going to meet all of your needs according to His riches in glory by Christ Jesus." I felt electricity go all through me! The next morning was the first morning I can remember having no money at all. As I checked my mail, I found a letter from a friend back home. He said, "Bill, I heard you left home to follow Jesus. I felt led to send you this." It was a check for forty dollars...enough for another week's rent at the YMCA at that time plus a little extra.

To make a long story short, the Lord had me wait until I truly fell in love with Him and was twenty-nine years old before He entrusted me with one of His daughters. When I had run out of money and began to see the Lord meet my needs in miraculous ways, it was then that I found my wife, my greatest miracle since salvation.

Dagmar and I met through circumstances connected with the prison ministry. I would bring inmates on work release home with me on weekends to stay at my apartment. I did not know that Dagmar's father, Earl, was visiting one of the inmates, Barry, who was staying with me one weekend. Earl invited Barry to dinner at their home, and since I was hosting Barry, he invited me also. At that dinner, I met my beautiful wife-to-be. After dating about a year and a half we got married with no money but on God's promise to provide.

Two months before our wedding date, I was singing in a little country church in Winchester, Virginia, with Brother Ben Murray preaching. After the service, a young man came up and asked Brother Ben if he knew of anyone who needed a bedroom suite. He said that he and his wife had it in the paper to sell but it wasn't selling and they felt they were supposed to give it away to bless someone. Brother Ben shared with him the next day that I was getting married in two months and that we were trusting the Lord to provide for everything. I had no furniture or anything of my own because it all belonged to the landlord where I was renting. The next week, the bedroom suite was delivered to my apartment. It was a three-piece solid cherry bedroom suite!

That same man called me a week later. He asked if I would come down to Winchester to visit him with my wife-to-be. He and his wife were both school-teachers and they had a beautiful home. As we talked, they began to share with us that God was calling them out west to go to Bible school and that they couldn't take everything with them. In fact, they felt led to trust the Lord to provide for them as they went out there. Besides that, they said, "God has spoken to us to give you everything in our house!" We thought we were dreaming! I said to Dagmar, "If this is a dream, don't wake me." They really did give us everything, from the washer and dryer down to the cereal boxes in the cupboards!

Our apartment couldn't hold everything, so we had to give certain things away. I said, "Lord, You have gone overboard to bless us!" The Lord said, "No, Bill, it's you! When you obeyed My voice to give your dream away, My Word promised that it would be given back to you—*pressed down, shaken together and running over shall men give into your bosom.*" We had received so much more than what "my" money in the bank account, which I had given away, would have gotten us.

Three

"You Are Going to Disney World!"

It seemed that the Lord began to speak to me little by little through everyday life and through situations in my family. I am convinced the Lord has to work in my life in this way or I would probably miss hearing Him. My children have taught me more than I have ever taught them. Just through their childlike spirit and faith I have been convicted over and over again of my lack of really trusting and believing God for the impossible.

One morning when our son, Joel, was seven years old, he told us that he had a dream that he went to Disney World. I have learned, after having two teen-age daughters, not to move my lips when my children mention anything about their dreams and plans. If I do, they will tell me the next day, "Daddy, you promised." So I didn't comment to Joel about his dream.

I told Dagmar that night, "Disney World is in Florida. We are in Maryland. I would never want to drive that far." I personally don't like to travel; that's probably why God called me into an international traveling ministry. "And we could never afford plane tickets for us to fly there, so just let the boy dream. It won't hurt him." But Joel started to pray, and he continued to pray for two whole years.

Two years later, my wife and I were invited to a leaders' conference at Brownsville Assembly of God in Pensacola, Florida. They told us that if we financed our way down, they would take care of the expenses once we got there, but we needed to let them know right away since there were only twenty seats left. How many of you have had a window of opportunity open up for you and you had to make a quick decision and you said yes—until you priced the plane tickets?

I started to have honest doubts about this trip because of the cost of the plane tickets. As I was in the kitchen one evening sharing with my wife, I said, "You know I am used to the Holy Spirit leading us, and I have learned that the devil usually rushes us to make a quick decision so we will miss the Lord." I said, "To be honest, I don't know if this trip is of God or of the devil."

My older daughter, Naomi, home that weekend from Bible college, was sitting in the living room overhearing her father, a great man of faith, doubting. Naomi walked into the kitchen and said, "Dad, do you think the devil would want you to go to Brownsville, where a major move of God is taking place?" I said, "Honey, can you come home more often?" What wisdom God has given to my daughter!

We stepped out and bought the plane tickets. We flew down to the conference and had a great time. As we were sitting on board the airplane in Pensacola to come home, an announcement came over the intercom: "We are sorry, but we have overbooked this flight. If there is anyone on board who would like to fly three hours later, we will offer you a free round-trip ticket good anywhere in the U.S. or Canada for the next year. If you are interested, just reach up and push the overhead service button." My hand shot up! I'll be honest—I don't pray about everything! I pushed anything that looked like a button. I didn't know there were so many gadgets above my head on an airplane.

The stewardess came back the aisle and motioned for us to come off the plane. They gave us a free lunch, rebooked us for three hours later, and gave us two free ticket vouchers good for the next year. I said to my wife on the plane coming home, "I don't know where we are going, but we are going somewhere with these free tickets." I then discovered that God rides on airplanes. He spoke to me that very moment, "Bill, you are going to Disney World! This is the answer to your son's prayers for two years. Any questions?" (The Lord has messed up some of my best plans and dreams.)

A few months later I was sharing at a retreat in Pennsylvania about how the Lord is honoring Joel's faith and moving on his dream and about how his faith is teaching me to trust God more. A lady came up to me after the meeting and said, "Brother Bill, I am on vacation up here. I live in Florida. I think when you get down there you are going to find that things are more expensive than you figured. She stood there and wrote out a check for five hundred dollars for Joel's trip. (My kids get bigger offerings than I do…most of the time.)

Two months later I was ministering in a church in Philadelphia, Pennsylvania, on Father's Day. I was sharing again about the faith of my children and about Joel's trip coming together. After the service, a man came up to me and introduced himself. He said, "Brother Bill, I am up here visiting a friend. I work at Disney World in Florida." We talked a little and then he left. The next day I went to pick up the offering from the pastor. The pastor said, "Bill, someone put this envelope in the offering basket at the end of the service yesterday morning." I opened the envelope and there were free passes to Disney World! How many of you know if God wants you to go someplace, it's impossible for you not to get there? Joel even let us go with him!

We had a great time at Disney World. Getting on board the plane to fly home, I whispered into Joel's ear, "Next time, we ought to go to Epcot." He's praying...and I'm getting ready! Oh, to have the faith of a child. No wonder Jesus said that unless we humble ourselves and become as children, we will never see His Kingdom, which is far better than Disney World.

Four

WE ARE WIRED DIFFERENT

My younger daughter, Danielle, who is a little strong-willed, and twenty-one as I am writing this, called me a few weeks ago. She said, "Dad, I bought a new car, a 2003 Honda Civic!" I said, "What? Honey, you just bought a nice Honda Civic two years ago. That car would last you forever! Besides that, your sister Naomi is getting married in May and then you will have to pay all the rent for your apartment plus this higher car payment each month. This is the worst time for you to do something like this."

She said, "I think I can handle it." Then before we hung up she said something that really floored me. She said, "I got a five-speed!" I said, "You are joking, right?" I said, "Honey, you have never driven a stick in your whole life!" She said, "I practiced with a friend's car yesterday afternoon."

I have come to this conclusion about Danielle—she is wired different! She is so unique. I believe that's the word of knowledge the Lord gave me concerning her. I have discovered something from the day she was born. She's an edge pusher! What worries me excites her. She was born to push the edge back.

She came two days later to show us her car. She parked two blocks away so she didn't have to park between any cars. I thought to myself, "She is probably going to be walking more since she got this new car!" As we looked it over, my wife said something that caused an alarm to go off inside of me. My wife asked, "Are you going to take us for a ride?" I went to get in the backseat, but Danielle spoke up and said, "Dad, I got a two-door this time." (The last time she bought a car, she wouldn't get one unless it was a four-door.)

She pulled out of the parking space slowly, squealing the tires. The next stop gave us another squeal that concerned me. She said, "Dad, I think it's because you are in here!" I wanted to say, "May I get out?" The longest ride in my whole life was just those two miles!

The Lord speaks to me in everyday life many times through my children. When you begin to hear God speak in everyday life, it can become very expensive. This word that the Lord spoke to me concerning you who are reading this book is costing my daughter over fifteen thousand dollars! So listen very carefully. I heard Him say concerning you, "You are so unique! You are wired different! Average just won't do it for you either. You're an edge pusher! You were born to push back the edge of the powers of darkness over your family, city, region and beyond."

I believe the Lord is taking the Body of Christ this hour into a dimension of the Spirit of a brand new Honda Civic five-speed! I believe the five-speed transmission represents the fivefold ministry of the apostle, prophet, pastor, teacher and evangelist.

People will shake their heads on this move and think you are going over the edge, but you were born to push the edge back and take great risks and do great exploits in this hour.

I sense we are going to hear some screeching of tires on this move. We will hear some squealing of people also who may not understand what God is up to. (By the way, I don't understand either. That's what makes it so exciting!) But God is in the car. He doesn't get nervous in the service like I do. He is going to teach you and me how to shift those gears to have all the power we need to do what He has called us to do corporately as well as individually. Did you know that Hondas are in the Bible? In the book of Acts it says that they were all in "one Accord."

This move is nothing new to God. He's been in a Honda before. He is calling us to get into "one Accord" so He can drive and shift for us.

Five

"You May Need to Be Adjusted"

I have been in the same church for thirty years at the time of this writing. I know there are times when the Lord leads us out of one church into another, but I believe that in most cases we leave on our own. I have been crucified several times in my own church concerning my gifting and calling. But I have discovered that where you get crucified is not very far from where God raises you from the dead and confirms your calling.

Many times during these thirty years the Lord has used those in authority over me and the members around me to reach out to give me advice concerning my prophetic gifting. I did not realize at the time that this was the Lord. I thought it was just man messing with me and my gift. I would take it personally and think they must not like me. I would get hurt and offended. Later on, I learned that this is how the Lord sharpens us. He uses iron to sharpen iron, stones to smooth stones, and people to grind people.

Have you ever seen a picture on a wall hanging a

little crooked? Is there anything wrong with that picture? There is nothing wrong with the picture itself—it just needs to be adjusted to show its beauty more gracefully. Have you noticed that a picture cannot adjust itself? And neither can we. God uses the people around us to reach out to touch our gifts and callings to ultimately bring out the best in us for Jesus to be seen.

The Lord gave me revelation on this. He said, "Bill, there is nothing wrong with your gift; it is from Me and it's a perfect gift. And there is nothing wrong with you. You are complete in Christ. But you may need to be adjusted!" I learned through time not to take it personally when the Lord would use someone to reach out and give advice and constructive criticism to me concerning my gift or calling.

The grinding we receive from other people sharpens us and our gifts. I wouldn't mind it if God used someone perfect in my life to adjust me. But God has chosen for some reason the most "unusual" people in my life to do that. (I could describe these people in more detail, but I would lose the anointing!)

We must realize that more than just refining our gift and calling, the Lord is out to conform us to His image. Can you think of someone right now whom you know was born to grind you and irritate you and rub you the wrong way? You actually need that person in your life! (If you can't think of anyone, I have a list of names that I would be glad to share with you.) No wonder God says to love even our enemies, for He often uses them to shape us and drive us closer to Him.

Six

I Wouldn't Have Chosen That Weapon

God is still using foolish things, this hour more than ever before. If He can use you and me, He can use anything and get away with it.

Several years ago I got a phone call one night from a sister at our church who was in charge of a citywide Young Messiah Celebration and she asked me an unusual question. She said, "Bill, Rabbi Ted Simon, who was going to carry the shofar down the aisle near the closing of the processional, cannot make the celebration after all." She said, "I was praying and felt led to ask if you would be willing to take his place and carry the shofar in the processional."

I felt honored. I said, "Yes." A shofar is a ram's horn, an instrument used by the Jews in the Old Testament. I had never touched one before, but I felt good about it. This was two weeks before the performance and I got to thinking. I said, "Lord, they used to blow these rams' horns in the Bible. They blew them at the walls of Jericho and the walls came tumbling down. Gideon's army blew them and the enemy got so confused that they committed suicide." I said, "Lord, it would be great if someone in our church could blow that thing." How many of you have ever looked for someone else to do something when God is looking for you to do it?

The Lord seemed to say, "Bill, you will be carrying it down the aisle and your lips will be the closest to it. Any questions?" Sometimes God really does make sense.

The Lord gave me His word on blowing it. He gave me the scripture where it says that *"the Spirit of the LORD came upon Gideon, and he blew a trumpet,"* which was a ram's horn (see Judges 6:34). I said, "Lord, if that same Spirit could come on me, I'd love to blow it." I scared my kids. I said to my daughters, "I just might take that shofar and blow it at the end of the Young Messiah Celebration!"

They said, "Dad, don't! Please don't! We are on the worship dance team coming down the same aisle behind you. Besides, we have friends in the youth group. Please don't blow it!"

Have you ever had to compromise with your children? I said, "Ok, I won't blow it…unless the Spirit of the Lord comes upon me!" When the Lord wants to do something, He has a way of preparing people for it. Besides, my daughters got over it pretty well.

The pastor dropped the shofar off to me an hour before the performance. I took the ram's horn into the prayer room. I wanted to see if I could blow it. I didn't even know how it was supposed to sound. As I put it up to my lips, I remembered something. I used to play a trumpet in the high school band many years ago. I wondered if it was the same technique. I put it up to my lips and blew, and out came a piercing blast of victory! The people in the church sanctuary said that when they heard it go off, they felt the presence of the Lord come into the sanctuary. A Jewish sister outside the prayer room shouted, "That's how it's supposed to sound! Take it and blow it at the end of the performance these two nights."

I opened the door to come out of the prayer room, and a visiting Jewish pastor turned and said to me, "Brother, would you be willing to come to our Feast of Tabernacles this fall and blow that shofar? I have never heard one blown that loud and clear!" I got my first invitation after my first blowing, and I still don't know what I am doing. All I know is that God said blow! I blew the shofar both nights during the processional and people were blessed.

How many of you have stepped out by faith and obeyed the Lord but you were glad when it was over? God spoke to me, saying, "Bill, it's not over! It's just begun. I want you to take this thing that appears foolish and I want you to start blowing it into households. I'm going to bring walls down inside of households and between family members this hour. Walls are coming down!"

I said, "Lord, I want to know something first. When the Spirit came upon Gideon and he blew the shofar, was that Gideon blowing or was that You?" The Lord spoke, "When Gideon blew his, I blew Mine! But it will work a little differently for you. When you blow it, it will be Me blowing because I live in you! When you blow into one end, My breath will literally come out the other!"

I personally believe that when I blow the shofar, His breath penetrates the darkness and blows into the lives of His people, bringing walls down!

I believe the Lord is raising up the shofar in this last hour to get us used to hearing that sound. For when the trumpet of the Lord blows, it will be the last sound out of here! Jewish people believe that the trumpet in Heaven is not a Louis Armstrong trumpet; it's a ram's horn! It could be called a Lamb's horn. Someone who died and went to Heaven and then came back to life testified to seeing the Shofar of the Lord, and said that it's fifteen miles long! When it blows, the dead in Christ down through the generations will hear it and be raised! I believe that every time a shofar is blown the enemy trembles, not knowing if it's that last trumpet sound!

You never know when you say yes to the Lord where it will take you. Many wait to do something big or miraculous, but the Lord will oftentimes test us by asking us to do something seemingly insignificant or even foolish. I never dreamed when I said yes to carry the shofar down that aisle that it would carry me across this nation, including Hawaii, and on two free trips to Israel just to blow the shofar. I've blown it on the Mount of Olives and at the Eastern Gate.

Many times the Lord will nickname the ram's horn as I travel to various places. What He nicknames it is what His breath will accomplish when it's blown. At the Pearl Harbor anniversary some years ago with permission from authority I blew it during the memorial service. God nicknamed the shofar there "The Pearl of Great Price." For the nation of Israel, He nicknamed it "The Chariot of Fire." For the state of New Jersey, the Garden State, it was nicknamed "The Rototiller." For the city of Boston, it was "The Boston Strangler." All I know is that God said blow!

Seven

I'D WAIT A LIFETIME TO HEAR GOD SPEAK

When I first got saved, my Bible teacher mentioned that he heard the Lord speak to him. I thought, "He is really a nut. No one can hear God speak today." As I was going to sleep that night, a strange and curious thought began rolling around in my head: "What if you could?"

I couldn't shake that thought. I began to ponder, "If it really was possible to hear God speak, that would be so awesome!" The desire began to burn and grow on the inside of my heart, and this thought burst forth: "If it was possible, I would be willing to wait my whole life through just to hear God say one word!"

The Lord puts His desires in us to fulfill them to overflowing. Little by little, I am still learning to hear Him. At times, I have missed hearing His voice, but I have heard it enough to get up when I have missed Him and keep going. When He speaks, the storm clouds scatter. When He speaks, new life begins to rise. When He speaks, suddenly you have hope where there was no hope. When He speaks, all things become possible.

And sometimes when the Lord speaks, His words are intended for more than just ourselves—sometimes He calls us to speak His words to others. This is the calling He has given me. I would like to share some words and visions that I believe the Lord has given me to share with you. I know we see through a glass darkly, so I know these words are only a part of the bigger picture. I pray that in some way they will encourage you and even impart into you an ear to hear for yourself what God is saying.

PART TWO

FROM THE
THRONE
OF GOD

One

I Saw Gold Pens Falling From Heaven

*And there are also many other things which Je-
sus did, the which, if they should be written
every one, I suppose that even the world itself
could not contain the books that should be
written. Amen.* John 21:25

I saw gold pens falling out of Heaven onto the earth
as though they were being thrown like javelins by the
angels into the hands of unknown people. I saw these
pens turning into spears and swords as they fell into
these hands. As their fingers began to write, books,
songs and poetry were becoming lethal weapons to
war against the enemy!

Psalm 144:1 was being activated throughout the
earth: *"Blessed be the Lord my strength, which teacheth
my hands to war, and my fingers to fight."*

In the Spirit, I saw huge warehouses in Heaven that
appeared to be full of books, songs and poetry. I no-

ticed these books had no titles on their covers or any words written on their pages. These were wordless books, blank bundles of sheet music and empty pages of poetry stacked high to the ceiling. A sign was posted over the huge door that read: "STATIONERY TO BE RELEASED AND PUBLISHED IN THE LAST FINAL HOUR UPON THE EARTH."

I heard the Father give a command to the angels: "Empty those warehouses and deliver the contents to the earth! There are books yet to be written, new songs yet to be sung, poetry yet to be recited that will woo hearts back to Me. Drop the pens down first and empty those warehouses."

I heard the Father say, "I'm releasing a scribe anointing upon the earth!"

In the Spirit, I saw as though the Grand Canyon itself was becoming one of the many distribution centers filling up like a huge library in the earth with testimonies, books, songs and poems. Then angels would swoop down and carry these writings to God-given destinations, to saints and sinners in many parts of the earth. I saw the seas and waters of the earth being covered with writings and literature floating upon them. The glory of God upon these waters from the writings would actually change water currents and carry them to places where man was unable to go.

I sensed the Lord Himself was going into marketing His material that He was releasing to the earth into hands that were being inspired to write by the Holy Spirit. I sensed the Father had a great desire to literally fill the earth to let the whole world know what great things He has done for His people.

"The LORD gave the word: great was the company of those that published it." Psalm 68:11 was being fulfilled.

Is there a book in you? A song stirring in your heart? Poetry that keeps coming to the surface? Perhaps the Lord is calling you this hour to pick up your pen!

Two

The Prisons Hold God's Treasures

It was late and I was tired, wanting to go to sleep, but God wanted to talk. It was about midnight, but it dawned on me that God does not sleep. His question made me restless: "Bill, where on earth does man keep his most priceless treasures and valuables?" I said, "Lord, usually these treasures, like gold, silver, diamonds and precious jewels, are kept locked up somewhere out of sight, usually with guards and other security measures to keep them under lock and key."

God spoke: "Like man's, My most valuable treasures on earth are also locked up."

I then saw Jesus standing in front of seemingly thousands of prisons and jails. The Lord said, "These have almost been destroyed by the enemy, but these ones have the greatest potential to be used and to bring forth glory to My name.

"Tell My people I am going this hour to the prisons to activate the gifts and callings that lie dormant in these lives that were given before the foundation of the earth. Out from these walls will come forth an army of spiritual giants who will have power to literally kick down the gates of hell and overcome satanic powers that are holding many of My own people bound in My own House.

"Tell My people that great treasure is behind these walls in these forgotten vessels. My people must come forth and touch these ones, for a mighty anointing will be unleashed upon these for future victory in My Kingdom. THEY MUST BE RESTORED." I then saw the Lord step up to the prison gates with a key. One key fit every lock, and the gates began to open.

I then heard and saw great explosions that sounded like dynamite going off behind the walls. It sounded like all-out spiritual warfare. Jesus turned and said, "Tell My people to go in now and pick up the spoil and rescue these." Jesus then began walking in and touching inmates who were thronging Him. Many being touched instantly began to have a golden glow come over them. God said to me, "THERE'S THE GOLD!" Others had a silver glow around them. God said, "THERE'S THE SILVER!"

In slow motion they began to grow into what appeared to be giant knights in armor—like warriors. They had on the entire armor of God, and every piece was solid and pure gold. Even their shields were made of gold. When I saw the golden shields, I heard God say to these warriors: "Now go and take what Satan has taught you and use it all against him. Go and pull down the strongholds coming against My Church."

These spiritual giants then started stepping over the prison walls with no one to resist them, and they went immediately to the very front line of the battle with the enemy. I saw them walk right past the Church as big-name ministers known for their power with God were surpassed by these giant warriors like David going after Goliath! They crossed the enemy's line and started delivering many of God's people from the clutches of Satan while demons trembled and fled out of sight at their presence.

No one, not even the church, seemed to know who these spiritual giants were or where they came from. All you could see was the armor, the golden armor of God from head to foot, and the shields of gold were there. The shields were restored to God's House and there was great victory and rejoicing. I also saw silver, precious treasures and vessels being brought in. Beneath the gold and silver were the people that nobody knew: THE REJECTS OF SOCIETY, STREET PEOPLE, THE OUTCASTS, THE POOR AND THE DESPISED. These were the treasures that were missing from His House.

In closing, the Lord said, "If My people want to know where they are needed, tell them they are needed in THE STREETS, THE HOSPITALS, THE MISSIONS AND THE PRISONS. When they come there, they will find Me and the next move of My Spirit and they will be judged by My Word in Matthew 25:42-43: *"For I was an hungered, and ye gave me no meat: I was thirsty, and ye gave me no drink: I was a stranger, and ye took me not in: naked, and ye clothed me not: sick, and in prison, and ye visited me not."*

Three

WEDDING BELLS IN THE SYNAGOGUES

I heard wedding bells beginning to ring inside Jewish synagogues in Israel and being amplified in the Spirit around the world. These bells immediately set off an alarm throughout the earth, causing principalities, strongholds and wicked spirits in high places to scream out, "This wedding cannot be! We have put a veil over the eyes and minds of His beloved so they are blinded from the truth! They will never believe He is their Messiah!"

But as these wedding bells kept ringing, I heard a demon cry out, "What about their ears? This sound is bypassing their minds and starting to woo their hearts! What if they start believing in their hearts through the hearing of these bells? Since faith comes by hearing God, we are sunk if this sound coming from Him has even a tiny mustard seed of faith in it!"

I heard the Lord proclaim to the angels that were standing at the four corners of the earth, "Begin to bring Me My beloved Bride. She is the one with the veil over her eyes."

Angels began to walk this beloved Bride-to-be down the aisles of every nation. For this wedding, His chosen people, the Jews, the apple of His eye, were seemingly getting His attention first. For this spiritual Bride coming forth to this wedding — like a natural bride — had a veil covering her eyes. I sensed she was Jewish.

As she came closer, I noticed her veil was covering her entire face. I then could see this Bride was also of Arab descent. And then every tribe, tongue, people and nation could be seen as this Bride was coming out of every race, religion and tradition, being drawn to her Bridegroom.

In the Spirit the backdrop of this wedding appeared to be a Jewish synagogue. I sensed that the Bridegroom had requested a wedding in His own hometown.

This wedding was taking place in a time of war. As hatred increased against God's chosen people, the Jews, wedding bells rang all the more loudly as He was wooing His Bride to His side. War appeared to be one of the "wedding attendants" ushering His Bride down to the altar to give herself totally to Him with no distractions or fear.

I then heard the Father whisper to the Bridegroom, His Son, "You may now lift the veil and kiss the Bride."

This veil was being lifted off the Jewish people first and then off the Arab people. Then multitudes without number from every race, tribe and nation were being kissed and swept off their feet as He ushered them into the bridal chamber.

In closing, I heard Jesus declare as wedding invitations were being sent out, "I am coming very soon for My Bride. Prepare for the wedding!"

I'll be home with bells on!

Four

ANGELS AT THE EASTERN GATE

In the Spirit, I saw two strong angels standing one on each side of the Eastern Gate of the city of Jerusalem, the same gate through which Jesus will make His entrance (grand finale) when He returns to set up His Kingdom. I sensed at first that these angels were standing in anticipation of His return, but then I knew in the Spirit that these angels with their arms extended were actually beckoning God's people, the Jews, to come home where they belong. A homesick feeling ordained of God was beginning to come into Jewish hearts, and they began aching and longing for their homeland.

I had a knowing also that before Jesus comes in His resurrected body through the Eastern Gate, these welcoming angels were beckoning and putting out a red-carpet greeting for the Body of Christ at large to come also. At such a crucial time in Israel, when fear would keep most of the Body of Christ from coming, these strong angels had been sent to welcome the Christ in us to come through the gates of Jerusalem as a prophetic sign of our soon-coming King.

As they seemed to be waving to the Body of Christ to come into the city, I heard the angels speaking to the hearts of believers who would come to love and serve and support the apple of God's eye. It was as though Jesus wanted to come home through His Body on earth to touch His people before He actually would return in His resurrected body, for He just could not wait to be with them again. He wanted to come now through His Body of believers on the earth.

I sensed these angels had begun to call many churches, pastors and believers by name to come visit Israel, but like Gideon's call, only the ones who were not fearful in the time of war and the ones who had faith through hearing God's voice through the angels were being chosen to go.

I sensed great excitement in Heaven as this invitation was being sent out through the angels.

It was like we were being given the once-in-a-lifetime opportunity to see Jesus face-to-face on earth as we would look into the eyes of His chosen people, the Jews, to bless them. His heart was beating faster at the very thought of this invitation. What we would do for His people we would be doing to Him!

I sensed that a greater blessing than we could imagine was going to come to our own homelands if we obeyed this call. I sensed the Lord saying, "If you visit My city and the people of My nation, I will visit you in your cities and establish your borders again."

I saw the red carpet being rolled out from the gates of the city of Jerusalem. I sensed the color red was representing the blood of Jesus that would be upon our feet as we would walk where Jesus once walked. I sensed the greatest fear in Israel was really coming from the devil himself. I could hear him saying with trembling as we entered the city, "Whose footsteps are those that I hear? They sound awfully familiar to me!"

Five

LAUNCHING PRAYER ROCKETS INTO ISRAEL

I saw strong angels standing wing tip to wing tip on the borders of Israel. Momentarily I saw a small break appear in a demonic black cloud that was hanging over the nation of Israel. As the small break in this cloud appeared, simultaneously the borders of Israel lit up like a flashing green light from Heaven signaling: "WE'VE GOT A GO FOR LAUNCHING!"

Immediately I saw many of these strong angels being released from their duty on the borders of Israel and being sent as in an emergency or a crisis to personally deliver messages to churches all over the world to pray for the peace of Jerusalem.

As pastors and churches received this call, I saw in the Spirit church sanctuaries turn into launching pads as fervent prayers increased. The intense, agonizing prayers with fasting began to shape what appeared to be rockets on launching pads. These rockets had the words "DESTINED FOR ISRAEL" written all over them.

As the burden of the Lord for Israel increased within these people, strong crying out could be heard to the heavens. I then saw these prayer-rockets being ignited and launched with fiery liftoffs and then shooting forth, being guided by Holy Ghost radar into the belly navel of the world—Jerusalem, Israel.

Not only were prayers sent through these churches, but I then saw some of these intercessors begin standing on the launching pads themselves and the Lord beginning to launch them like SWAT teams for secret missions as though their prayers were launching them also over into Israel.

This is the *kairos* moment for Israel to be interceded for and a now-or-never moment for the Body of Christ at large to respond.

Six

SHEKINAH GLORY OVER JERUSALEM

In the Spirit, I heard such violent intercession for Israel ascending from the earth that the very foundations of Heaven were being shaken through these relentless cries.

The culmination of tears, prayers and worship seemed to release a new sound vibrating the heavens, causing an avalanche of angels to suddenly appear upon the walls of Jerusalem!

The angels upon the walls kept looking upward proclaiming...

> *"Lift up your heads, O ye gates; and be ye lift up, ye everlasting doors; and the King of glory shall come in. Who is this King of glory? The LORD strong and mighty, the LORD mighty in battle.... The LORD of hosts, he is the King of glory."*
>
> Psalm 24:7-8, 10

A cloud of Shekinah glory appeared, hovering over

Jerusalem. I then saw a huge shofar as though it was being pushed down through this cloud of glory towards the earth, as though it was about to be blown.

As this huge shofar pierced through the cloud of glory, divine revelation began to be released upon Jerusalem. The goodness and the kindness of the Lord was pouring out of this cloud upon His people.

Out of the shofar, God's voice began to be heard as of a trumpet talking with His people. I then realized the Lord would use the shofar to speak forth His voice to His people before it would be blown from Heaven.

I heard God's voice flowing out of the end of this huge shofar into the ears and hearts of His chosen people. One word especially began to resonate throughout the whole earth...

"LIFT UP YOUR HEADS! YOUR REDEMPTION DRAWETH NIGH!"

Seven

JEWISH ROOTS SURFACING IN CHURCHES WORLDWIDE

As we were crying out for Israel, I saw Jewish roots as though watered by tears begin to surface in churches throughout the world. As the Body of Christ prayed for the peace of Jerusalem, we discovered by revelation that we were a "piece" of Jerusalem. Our very roots were Jewish. We were Jewish on our Father's side. Israel was our home. We can sing, "This land is your land, this land is my land from the Mount of Olives to the Golan Highlands. From the Dead Sea waters to the Hill Golgotha, this land was made for you and me."

As these roots grew and wrapped around our hearts, we were finding our true identity in Christ, and His compassion began to explode in our hearts for His chosen people—the Jews. Our heart's desire and prayer for Israel was that they might be saved.

As churches discovered and embraced these roots, these roots brought revelation and blessing into the lives of the people. Churches began to be rooted and grounded in a dimension of God's love that they had not known before. These churches that embraced their Jewish roots ended up with the whole Tree of Life in their midst!

I heard the Lord say, "I will bless them that bless Me. And those that bless My people (the Jews) will find a Jewish carpenter building their church!"

Eight

"Call Forth the Minstrels
Upon the Earth"

In the Spirit, I heard angelic choirs singing as
though they were rehearsing for the last time in
Heaven before they would join the worshipers on
earth for what seemed to be the grand finale of the
worship of all the ages that would bring the glory of
God to fill the earth.

I saw a huge curtain like a veil that separated the
earth from the glory of Heaven. A strong angel was
holding onto a rope that he was about to pull to open
this curtain that would flood the earth with Heaven's
glory.

But I heard the King of Glory say, "Not yet! Call forth
the minstrels upon the earth to begin to sing and worship Me, for My choirs of angels and angelic bands
are now ready to join in with them. Bring Me a minstrel, and the earth will hear from Heaven! The earth
will begin to hear My voice as I step forward to sing
solo as they worship together, backing me up as an

orchestra, worshiping in Spirit and in truth. I will romance the earth with songs of love that were written before the foundations of the earth."

I then saw heavenly sheet music being released from on high with words and music that were out of this world, distributed by angels to minstrels upon the earth. There were songs of deliverance, healing, salvation and resurrection. The dead would hear these songs of glory.

When these songs were sung, there would be instant power going into people's hearts and minds and bodies. Instant deliverance with everlasting victory would change the saints and sinners forever. Oh, what glory I am seeing right now. "O for a thousand tongues to sing my great Redeemer's praise, the glories of my God and King, the triumphs of His grace." It is literally on its way to earth!

I heard the Father say, "Let everything that has breath praise the Lord!" Breathing alone was the qualifying factor for us to be worshipers in this last hour. If you are breathing, God is calling you to worship. We are being called to be full-time worshipers—part-time anything else.

I could now see that everyone that had breath was a minstrel and was being ordained by God to praise Him, causing God to arise and His enemies to scatter as His glory invades planet earth. I saw mountains being called to break forth into singing and the trees of the field to clap their hands. Even birds were being ordained to sing in this choir of worshipers! Everything that had breath was being summoned to appear before God Almighty to praise Him.

An old song was being rewritten in glory: "Saul has slain his thousands and David his ten thousands." And now the tabernacle of Davidic worship being built on the earth will witness the powers of the enemy being slain by mass destruction.

In closing, the Lord said, "The curtain of the veil of My glory will be ripped from top to bottom, and as truly as I live, all the earth will be filled with the glory of the Lord. The very first note and word of the first song of corporate worship will split that veil. Call forth every minstrel in Heaven and earth. Their practice and rehearsal days are now over. Their time to sing a new song to Me has now come. And My time to sing My love songs to them is here.

"I'm rending the heavens and descending to earth upon the wings of worship!"

Nine

OUR WORSHIP BREAKS THE
SPIRITUAL SOUND BARRIER

I heard the Lord speak to a strong angel, saying, "Turn up the sound of worship on the earth." The sound of our worship was being amplified in the Spirit. The sound of dancing feet in just one church was amplified—making it sound to the enemy as if a million worship dancers had come to town.

The sound of shofars blowing was magnified, sounding like Gabriel's trumpet to the enemy's ears. As God's people were worshiping, I heard a spiritual sound barrier being broken in the Spirit realm in heavenly places. A corporate anointing coming upon His Body had increased in such a manner that it had launched our worship like a rocket being shot into the heavens with great force.

I sensed strongly that a great spiritual barrier had been broken in the heavenlies. At first I thought it was a barrier that had held back our worship from going all the way to the throne room, but now I realized the Lord had been hearing us sing unto Him in worship all along. The fact is we had not been able to hear Him sing! I sensed the breaking of the barrier would now enable us not only to hear the Lord sing but to actually have Him sing with us. He had long been singing *over* us with joy, but now He would be coming down to sing *with* us, producing a new sound the earth has never heard.

His angelic choir led by His beautiful voice was now beginning to be heard as it was descending and mixing with our voices in worship filling the earth.

The whole earth was like a concert hall, hearing worship that sounds out of this world, but now coming into the world. Songs of salvation, healing and deliverance were breaking forth with awesome power coming upon the earth as the Lord Himself joined in worship with His Body, releasing a new sound through worship. Even the mountains and the hills were breaking forth into singing, and the trees of the field were clapping their hands.

Ten

MANY WORSHIPERS HANG UP
THEIR HARPS

I heard the Lord say, "Many whom I have called into deep intimate worship of loving Me, the King of kings and Lord of lords, soon will be tested as they are called upon to stand before My kings of the earth—the pharaohs, the King Sauls and many shepherds whose hearts have been hardened.

"If these worshipers will stand still and worship Me in the midst of these ones I have placed in authority for My purposes and know that I am God, I will be exalted in the earth and among the heathen and even in My own House."

Worship will take you farther than you want to go.

I sensed the Lord saying to the angels when King Saul was ruling over Israel and losing his kingdom…"I keep hearing worship coming up from the hillsides of Judea from a shepherd boy. He is absolutely lost in worshiping Me. He's a full-time worshiper and a part-time shepherd." I heard the Lord say to the angels, "Kill any enemy that comes against his flock of sheep—any bear, lion or giant—for anything that interrupts his worshiping Me has to die. Any questions?

"I have found a worshiper who is so lost in Me that even the wrong authority over him and his people does not distract him. He has learned to worship Me in secret in the midst of those stinking sheep. I have found the next king of Israel. Tell Samuel to go anoint him!"

God looks for a worshiper when He wants to change things in His Kingdom.

As David was anointed by Samuel, the Spirit of the Lord came upon him from that day forward…and the Spirit of the Lord departed from Saul. (This could have been a good time for David to celebrate the downfall of a leader—but David, a true worshiper, didn't think so.)

In Saul's torment, he called for his servants to seek out a man who was a cunning player on a harp and bring him to him. *"And David came to Saul, and stood before him: and he loved him greatly; and he became his armor-bearer"* (1 Samuel 16:21). Saul became refreshed as David stood before him worshiping God, and he was well whenever David played and the evil spirits departed from him.

I sensed the Holy Spirit whispering, "Don't write off every King Saul, pharaoh or shepherd whose heart is hardened. For the heart of the king and every man is in My hand and like a river I am able to turn their hearts in whatever direction I choose. You never know when a Saul will become a Paul, when a pharaoh may become a Moses, or when a shepherd with a hardened heart will become a lover of My sheep.

"There is enough power in just one worshiper who

allows Me to love through them to change the course of history in My Kingdom. I am seeking this hour for worshipers—even just one—who will allow Me through them to influence the hearts of leadership in My Kingdom and in the world."

I sensed the Lord saying, "I have already prepared worshipers for this hour who are so sensitive to My Spirit that even silent worship with their everyday lives will ultimately open up hearts of authority over them."

David's greatest enemy was not the lion, bear or giant. His greatest enemy was in the House of God, and time and again God reminded him: "You can't touch this!" David knew somehow that Saul was still God's anointed even though he didn't act like it. God many times uses the Sauls in our lives to prepare us for a great destiny.

Get ready to take your harp off the weeping willow tree. Our God is calling many in this hour to stand beside our Sauls, pharaohs and shepherds whom we may not like. But don't stop worshiping now. You have come too far to turn back. Take your harp down now. God protected David because he was born to worship, and so were you. Ongoing worship will shield you and heal your wounds from past hurts from pharaohs, Sauls and shepherds. Healed people heal people.

True worship will cause our hands to be raised not only upward but also outward, like Jesus' hands were on the cross—the greatest display of worship to the Father that is still influencing multitudes today, even King Sauls, pharaohs and hurting shepherds.

Eleven

CORPORATE WORSHIP WREAKS HAVOC ON THE ENEMY

As streams of worship flowing out of different churches were coming together, I saw whole cities plunged beneath a great cleansing flood as darkness began pursuing God's enemies.

I heard the enemy scream at the flowing of these streams: "How can it be? Worship teams are breaking loose out of the boundaries of their own churches and flowing together corporately with other worship teams. We must stop their anointings from mixing together. Their strengths will be contagious to one another and their weaknesses will be drowned in the presence of their God as He inhabits their praises!"

Then the enemy complained, "Don't let them cross-pollinate!"

The enemy continued shouting orders to regroup his confused demons: "If they cross-pollinate, they will find honey in the rocky places of their own churches and personal lives. This is not the way it's supposed to be! We must increase our distractions to keep them separated and isolate them, consuming them with their own individual problems and personal struggles."

The enemy spoke again trembling, "Stop the flow! Stop the flow! We're losing focus. As they are flowing together, it's like they are moving in the Spirit and leaving no forwarding address! If they continue to come together, we will surely lose sight of them as they become one. And if we lose these churches through corporate worship, we will surely lose this city!"

In the Spirit, I heard chains snapping, fetters breaking and strongholds being demolished. Wicked spirits in high (governmental) places were weakening as corporate worship was rising higher—thrusting upward like a spiritual sword and severing the jugular vein of the prince of the power of the air over cities and regions.

Twelve

I Heard a War Cry—"Call for the Worship Dancers!"

In the Spirit, I saw a battlefield where the enemy had planted many land mines just beneath the surface of the ground. God's soldiers came onto the battlefield dressed in full armor and in what appeared to be extra-large combat boots. As they began to take a step forward, a strong command was shouted from the heavenlies: "Stop! You must not walk onto this battlefield. The hidden land mines are too dangerous!"

I then heard the Lord say to a strong angel, "Call for the worship dancers." I saw them coming. They didn't look like they were coming to fight a battle. They looked barefoot and happy. In fact, not even the angel told them about a war. They looked like they were just continuing to worship God, lost in His presence. They seemingly had come from out of nowhere. Most were small children who just enjoyed dancing with their angels near the front of churches on Sunday mornings. (Many parents thought it was cute to watch them try to enter into worship, but God was trying to use them to lead us to His throne.)

Some were youth and older ones, but the older ones seemed to feel intimidated by others and were not able to be free with a childlike spirit. The older the people got, the more war-minded they seemed to become. It seemed only the children knew how to worship and knew nothing of war because their pure, innocent worship *was* war without their even knowing it! In their Father's presence with their angels, they just didn't have time to think about anything being against them. They seemed to be living the word: "For if God be for us, who or what can be against us?"

They came, bare feet and all, uninhibited by strong soldiers talking about danger and the fear of losing their lives. They came dancing right onto the battlefield, seemingly deaf to the words of caution being given by the adult soldiers. (By the way, I cannot find the word *adult* in the whole Bible. It's only used in the word *adultery*. We are all children to Him.)

WORSHIP DETONATES THE LAND MINES OF THE ENEMY! Lost in the glory of God, these young dancers continued worshiping the Lord with their feet, taking more territory back from the enemy. As their feet danced upon the battlefield and touched down upon the hidden land mines, instead of exploding, these land mines just fizzled as though there were no explosives in them. Simultaneously, for every land mine these feet danced upon, many more land mines were detonated in the Spirit inside the enemy camp far away.

I then saw grown men and women starting to take

their huge combat boots off and start dancing, bringing the glory of God down onto this battlefield. Grown-ups were shouting, "Be careful where you walk; but if you dance, don't worry about anything! Rejoice in the Lord always, and again I say, rejoice!" (To rejoice literally means, to jump up and turn around in a dance.)

God was arising and His enemies were scattering, fleeing before us seven ways. The weapons of our warfare are not carnal (what we think), but they are mighty through God to the pulling down of strongholds!

Care to dance?

No more combat boots for me!

Thirteen

NEW WINE IS COMING TO MARRIAGES

Can you imagine the Father, Son and Holy Spirit meeting before the foundation of the world to decide when and where to release the very first miracle upon the earth through the ministry of Jesus? If I were Jesus, I probably would vote to raise someone from the dead at the very beginning so my ministry would never have to send out another newsletter.

I personally believe it was the shortest meeting ever with a unanimous decision: "Let's release the first miracle on earth where it will be needed the most: at a wedding feast so everyone will know they can have a miracle in their marriage."

Did you know that when God brought you and your spouse together, He knew you would need a miracle? In fact, there's something wrong if you don't need a miracle in your marriage. Couples in the Bible who had the greatest destiny seemed to face the greatest impossibilities in their marriages.

Abraham and Sarah were destined to conceive and

bring forth a son of promise. "But, Houston, we've got a problem! Sarah can't seem to get it together and conceive. Let's forget about this miracle stuff and get Hagar (another woman is what I need) to fulfill my destiny," Abraham thought, especially since Sarah thought of it first.

Both agreed to a man-made solution. Sarah admitted, "No, I don't have what it takes. Go ahead and have Hagar…. I am tired of this unfulfilled marriage." Through painful experiences, Abraham and Sarah learned that they needed more than each other (and a third party) to have their fulfillment in life.

Finally, they realized that their answer was not in each other. God waited until they both could not possibly have a child in the natural. Not only was Sarah's womb as dead as ever, but Abraham was about a hundred years old…out of commission also.

They finally had to take their eyes off of themselves and look to the Lord, realizing that it was a "mission impossible." God was waiting all those years to hear them say what He knew all along: "We need a miracle in our marriage!"

THE GREATER THE CALL ON A MARRIAGE, THE GREATER THE NEED FOR MIRACLES!

In the first chapter of Luke, Zachariah and Elizabeth had an impossible area in their marriage. There was a barren place in their marriage also. Elizabeth could not conceive. Zachariah was serving as a priest in the Temple and had the greatest experience of his life. The angel gave him the word of the Lord about his destiny of having John the Baptist for a son…representing the prophetic move coming to prepare the way of the Lord. *"As soon as the days of his ministration* [duties in the Temple] *were accomplished, he departed to HIS OWN HOUSE"* (Luke 1:23). Then his wife, Elizabeth, who had been barren, conceived! Many men today in the Temple, or ministry, are being called by God to return to their own houses to their own "barren" wives. Not until the men of God learn and experience spiritual intimacy with their own wives, so they can spiritually conceive, can couples fulfill God's purpose for marriage—to bring forth godly seed, children of destiny.

Our ministries can go no further than our marriages if we want children of destiny. It's really out of spiritual intimacy with our spouses that ministry is birthed. I sense husbands and wives will have to hold hands to bring forth the next move of the Spirit. Men will have to cleave to their wives because it will take two for what God wants to do next. God is coming to couples in their own houses this hour.

Many men and women have received great visions and words from the Lord in churches. But the real conception of these words must take place in our homes where we live. I want to say this carefully— the conception of my children did not take place in the church where I attend. Their conception took place in our home with my wife and me through intimacy. Spiritual conception must also take place in our homes if we are going to see our destiny fulfilled and the Kingdom of God advance. Have we men failed to take home what we received in God's House and neglected spiritual intimacy with our wives at home?

I sense that the wine (intimacy) has run out in

many marriages, but I hear the Lord saying to the angels, "Get the water pots and fill them with water. I'm going to turn water into wine again and marriages into miracles. I have saved My best wine that has been aging for centuries for this last hour. I have saved the best wine for last to be tasted right at home between husband and wife."

Is there spiritual barrenness in your marriage? Do you need a great miracle? Your great need for a miracle qualifies you to receive one.

Fourteen

THE SCEPTER IS UP FOR HUSBANDS AND WIVES TO PRAY TOGETHER

In the Spirit, I saw an open window in the heavens and a scepter rising up over husbands and wives, calling them to come boldly to the throne of grace in prayer together.

I sensed the Lord saying, "It's time to call for some of My most powerful intercessors on earth to release My power in unprecedented ways that have not yet been seen—the prayer power of agreement between a husband and a wife."

I suddenly became aware that when Jesus spoke of His House becoming a house of prayer, He was referring to your house and my house—right where we live. He was speaking right to the very core of His Church—husbands and wives. We are the house—His House—that He longs to live in and reign in.

In the Spirit, I saw valleys of decisions coming towards many families, churches and ministries. These decisions that soon needed to be made would affect not only our own lives, but the lives of generations to come. I saw the enemy releasing friction and strife between husbands and wives because of these upcoming landmark decisions. Satan's purpose was to lead the spouses to look for prayer elsewhere—from some other source—for he feared and knew that their coming together in agreeing prayer would dethrone the influence of his kingdom from their lives, families, churches, jobs and ministries.

I saw in the Spirit many men crying out to God in secret for help and for more strength in their lives, ministries and jobs. Surprisingly, the Lord spoke in a way that many men could not hear Him.

"I have already given you help. Where is your helpmeet? Ask her to pray for you. She is your most powerful intercessor on this earth."

As men were awakened and would ask their wives to pray, I saw the prayers of wives like lightning shooting upward to the throne room of God, pushing back demonic powers and bypassing the prayers of others that seemed to take forever to get answers. I then saw that our wives at times became the answer for us as the Lord would give them wisdom.

Sometimes our wives' voices would speak instead of God's. At other times the Lord would use the husbands the same way for the wives. But it all started as we would begin to pray not just for each other separately at a distance but as we physically together prayed and came into unity as we waited upon the Spirit to direct us even how to pray. Even in waiting together before the Lord in silence, we were discovering a rekindling of love that had grown cold between us and the Lord and each other.

I saw the Holy Spirit imparting His desires and prayers into husbands and wives around the world. As these spouses grew through praying together, becoming truly one in the Spirit, their spiritual intimacy began to influence whole families, churches, secular jobs, ministries and even nations.

As this scepter continued to rise higher, I heard Jesus say, "Whatever you ask the Father in My name He will give you, that I may be glorified in you. Even ask for that which you have been afraid to ask Me for in times past, for now is your time."

It seemed the closer these couples became through prayer, the closer God was. Praying in the Spirit together seemed to speed up the process to release the Lord's hands to do His perfect will and handcuff the enemy at the same time. As these spouses continued to pray together, their houses began turning into sanctuaries, healing homes and havens of deliverance.

You and your spouse were brought to the Kingdom for such a time as this. Your prayers together will get victories that you will not get any other way.

It's time to pray. Where is your spouse?

Fifteen

"I WILL ARREST YOUR LOVED ONES"

I sense the Lord saying, "As My people this hour come to Me and find *rest*, they will also find *restoration* taking place in their households. The name Noah means 'rest.' As Noah rested in Me, I worked through him to build the ark and into the ark of safety I brought his whole family. Many of My people are restless and are rocking the boat in their own households, causing family members to look elsewhere for security and peace. But as My people begin resting in My love for them, they will discover that that rest will be contagious.

"First Noah had rest. Then Noah's whole family found rest in the ark. Then even the animals were drawn there and found a resting place. Listen, if the animals got into the ark, your family can make it in.

"Then when the flood came, the ark started resting itself upon the flood waters. And when it was all over, the ark rested on Mount Ararat. The ark is still resting there today. Resting in My love for you will become the drawing power to draw your household to Me. But *rest* must come before *restoration*! Restoration begins with r-e-s-t!

"Rest also brings *revelation*. As My people rest in Me, revelation will break forth upon them, giving forth light to all that are in the house. I will reveal Myself to them."

It's like the Lord is saying to us, "If you rest, I will work. As you rest, I will arrest your loved ones by the Holy Ghost and bring them in. You cannot save them. You could not save yourself. I saved you. Let Me be their Savior too."

I sense that God is about to make personal house calls. He's coming in 3-D technicolor straight to your house. There is a rest to those who believe. And that rest will bring in your whole house. *"Believe on the Lord Jesus Christ, and thou shalt be saved, and thy house"* (Acts 16:31).

I see angels standing at attention with your personal address written on them. They are about to be released to set up camp round about where you live to begin delivering family members.

Houses will be turned into homes. Let's enter into God's rest so He can bring the rest of our households in.

Quit rocking the boat!

Sixteen

MOTHERS' PRAYERS ARE SHAKING THE DOOR HINGES OF HEAVEN

Angelic assignments were being given to bring in the "seed" of praying mothers.

In the Spirit, I saw a heavenly rush of angels gathering. Prayers of mothers crying out for their children seemed to be gathering momentum.

These prayers, as though being amplified in the Spirit, were pounding on and relentlessly shaking the door hinges of Heaven. Heaven itself had been shaken by these violent prayers, as though a bear had been robbed of its cubs.

I heard a loud voice from the throne shout to the angels: "Answer the front door! The bowl of prayers for children prayed by their mothers is now full and tipping over. Angels, receive your assignments!"

I then saw angels stand at attention while these names of children and their personal addresses were being written on them. Some were "on the street" addresses—unknown by man but known by God. There were also prison addresses. Even telephone numbers were being given out to some angels who would make person-to-person telephone calls on the earth to some of these children. Some assignments of angels were just to make phone calls and speak to their hearts things that nobody else knew.

On the streets, pay phones would ring and homeless children would be led to answer these phones and receive a call from Heaven!

Special assignments were given to many angels to come down and strengthen and comfort mothers.

I heard the Lord say to the angels, "Speak comfortingly to the mothers and say, 'Your warfare is accomplished. I will speak to the north to give them up and to the south to hold them back no longer. I will bring them from the east and west. I will save your children.'

"As for Me, this is My covenant with them," says the Lord. "My Spirit that is upon you, and My words which I have put in your mouth, shall not depart out of your mouth, nor out of the mouth of your seed, nor out of the mouth of your seed's seed from henceforth and forever," says the Lord. (See Isaiah 59:21.)

Seventeen

A Word to the Kingdom's Older Stars

As Cal Ripken stood up to the plate for his first time at bat in his final all-star game, he blasted the first pitch over the left field wall. On the heels of announcing his retirement, Cal Ripken broke the record and became the oldest player to hit a home run in an all-star game and was named MVP, most valuable player, in his last all-star appearance.

As history was made that night, I sensed the Lord saying, "The older stars in My Kingdom are going to shine brighter and do greater exploits than ever before."

I sense there is a special anointing coming upon older men and women in the Body of Christ. God is not through using you. Your age is not against you; it is for you! Job 12:12 says: *"With the ancient is wisdom; and in length of days understanding."*

You have more wisdom now than ever. With years comes understanding. This anointing is going to cause you to live longer. Many of you have not planned to live long enough! It will be an anointing similar to Caleb's when he was eighty-five years old and he said to Joshua, "I am as strong now as I was at forty, and I still want that mountain!"

There is coming a spiritual fountain of youth into your midst: a renewing, a release of God's strength. Psalm 68:28 says: *"Thy God hath commanded thy strength."*

God is commanding His strength into you!

Some of you are going to have to live longer because God is not through using you. Many of you are going to go into a second childhood in the Spirit. You will be reactivated by God to live out the dreams that you are now only dreaming about.

Other people and relatives will laugh and say, "You are going to do what? You are going to go where? At your age?" But that anointing is going to rise up within you to take mountains, to do exploits, to run and not be weary, to walk and not faint.

Our older years are when we are in our prime to be used and to bring forth fruit. Psalm 91:16 says: *"With long life will I satisfy him, and show him my salvation."* There is an anointing coming upon God's people to live longer. The joy of the Lord, which is our strength, is lengthening our days upon the earth.

Many have made out their wills, but before you think about leaving, check out your Father's will for you. I don't think you are going anywhere for a while. As Abraham and Sarah conceived in old age, you are about to conceive and live to see the birth of your Isaac—your *impossible dream.*

Eighteen

A Stump in the Field

I saw the Body of Christ plowing with great difficulty in the field of labor. Finally, our plow seemed to
hit a stump in the field and we couldn't go any farther. In spite of all our efforts and praying, this stump
remained unmovable and steadfast. Our hearts were
broken, for we knew God had placed us here to plow
in this great field of harvest. But this stump in the field
was stopping us.

I then heard the Lord say, "You have hit treasure!
This is no ordinary stump of an ordinary tree. You
have just hit the base of the tree of Calvary. It's the
cross growing in your field! You must not, I repeat,
you must not remove it. It is growing in your field to
remove you out of the way from hindering My harvest. You will have to embrace this cross and die before I can release resurrection power into your field
of labor."

As we beheld the cross growing in our field, we began to experience a severe pruning in our spiritual
giftings, especially in the area of the prophetic. He was
cutting and pruning us back to bring forth a more sure

word. He was adjusting our gifts, callings and ministries to bring forth the fruit of servanthood in our lives. I felt the Lord say, "Your giftings are showing more than your fruit. You are embarrassing Me!"

Then I remembered that right before nailing Him to the cross, they had beaten Jesus and had cried out to Him, "Prophesy to us!" But He didn't.

There are times when you don't prophesy; you just show others how to die—to self, giftings and plans.

As we embrace the cross, death and surrender will bring forth fruit that will remain to bring in the harvest. In fact, fruit is the harvest—it will bring it in. In Italy they have discovered that grapevines produce more fruit when grown on cross-like poles. They get more sunshine and fresh air.

Many in the Body are spiritually "stumped" in their lives, families and ministries in this hour. They feel they are at a crossroads and are looking for a fresh word from Heaven to tell them what to do. Many are asking, "Lord, should I go this way or that way?"

But I sense the Lord pointing to the cross and saying, "Go this way: spread out your arms." You are not at a crossroads; you are at the cross.

Have you been betrayed? You are nearing your cross.

Have you been rejected? You are getting closer.

Don't run away now. If you miss your crucifixion, you will miss your resurrection.

Nineteen

MURMURING AND COMPLAINING WERE LOCKING THE GATES

In the Spirit, I saw the King of Glory standing just outside the gates of many strategic cities in our nation and abroad. He was ready to come in through the gates with power and authority. But He could not. I then noticed that on the inside of the gates were huge locks with these words written on them:"Murmuring and Complaining."

I sensed the Spirit saying, "Murmuring and complaining coming from God's people has put a lock on the front gates of many cities, keeping the King of glory from entering in."

I heard the King of Glory saying as He stood in front of the gates, "Through their murmuring and complaining My people are saying, 'God is not able to meet our needs—let alone save our city!'

"Complaining and murmuring is really unbelief at its worst! If I came through the gates of many cities now, My hands would still be tied by unbelief in many hearts of My people. I could not do much. My glory inside of cities would soon fade because of unbelief. My Son faced the same problem when He entered His own hometown where people knew Him best, but He could not do many miracles because of their unbelief."

Once again, faith is locked outside the gates of many cities wanting in, and unbelief takes a city to prison.

I sensed the Lord saying, "My people must start believing now that I can save them and their city before I come in or their unbelief and doubt will stop Me when I do come in."

In the Spirit, I saw a key that would fit the lock that murmuring and complaining had put on the gates. The key had the word "THANKSGIVING" engraved on it. I heard the King of Glory say, "If My people will repent from their unbelief and draw nigh to Me and begin to enter My gates with thanksgiving, I will enter their gates with glory and great power.

"They must start right where they are and begin to thank Me that they are anywhere on this earth alive. I have spared their lives to praise and worship Me in this last hour, for their giving of thanks and praise and worship will become My strong habitation among them as I fight their battles through the weapon of worship. *In every thing give thanks: for this is the will of God in Christ Jesus concerning you* (1 Thessalonians 5:18). You must trust Me on this command."

As I began to hear a spirit of thankfulness rise up out of God's people in cities around the earth, I saw the Key of Thanksgiving turning in the locks on city gates and demonic powers fleeing as the King of Glory took a giant step through the gates to inhabit the praises of His people. Filling His people on the inside with His very self, He began to rise up within them and began to loose whole cities through them as they then began to send Judah (praise) first.

God was now entering the gates of our cities through thanksgiving in our hearts and entering our courts (dwelling places) through our praise to Him. We had become terrorists to the devil through our worship, which was the highest form of warfare. A great cloud of witnesses on high seemed to be joining in with angelic choirs singing, "Let God arise and His enemies be scattered!" and "Oh sing, you desolate cities, for you shall be inhabited!"

Twenty

CHAINS AND LOCKS ON OUR WALLETS

In the Spirit, I saw words coming out of the mouths of God's people that appeared to be forming chain-like links hooking together. These were negative words, and with each comment, the chain grew, wrapping itself around the object we were complaining about.

One of the largest chains I saw was wrapping around finances. Each time someone would say, "I don't have enough money," this chain became reinforced with strength, wrapping tighter around that person's wallet or purse. As this complaining continued, I saw huge locks come upon these chains, as a spirit of poverty and depression began to be released from hell to fulfill the words that were being spoken.

I saw enormous chains come over whole ministries and churches. Wherever two or more people were gathered together and began to say, "We don't have enough money for this or that in our ministry or church," huge chains began to wrap around whole ministries, congregations, pulpits and altar rails.

I saw a muzzle come over the mouths of many pastors when just a few church members spoke in agreement, saying, "We can't afford to pay him that much!" Chains from hell started growing around the pastor's whole family as the spirit of poverty continued to increase in churches, like a little leaven leavening the whole lump! I saw churches closing as chains and locks were being installed on their front doors as the spirit of poverty overcame many members, stopping them from giving tithes and offerings.

I then saw in the Spirit one person stand up in a church that was about to close its doors. This person began to lift up his wallet toward Heaven and began thanking God that he even had a wallet. Though nothing was inside his wallet, he began praising God that he had the breath to praise Him in spite of his lack of finances.

As this man started lifting up his wallet with thanksgiving and praise, the chain snapped off of it and the Lord spoke audibly to this church, "Let everything that has breath praise Me! In everything give thanks, for this is the will of God in Christ Jesus concerning you and this house." A revelation was breaking forth upon God's people that just breathing qualifies us to praise and worship Him.

"In God We Trust" became a sermon as someone pulled out his last dollar bill and began to read what was written on his money instead of counting how much he didn't have. God spoke: "Don't count your money—read it! Count on Me!"

As ministries, churches and their members discovered that God was their source, they were freed as the chains and locks began to melt in the presence of the Lord.

A fresh oil of giving flowed upon God's people as they became thankful. As they started thanking God for their wallets and purses even though they were empty and the people were needy, I saw a key being turned in the door of a bank in Heaven and finances from this bank beginning to fill wallets, purses, ministries and churches with whatever they needed. I saw the future of many churches—they were so blessed and prosperous from members giving freely that pastors had to announce to their congregations: "We have enough money. Please pray to see where God would have us use the extra finances that have come in."

It seemed that when God's people began to give thanks, they discovered blessings and finances they didn't know they had before. The money would come from somewhere, somehow, for their hearts of thanksgiving wanted to give instead of receive. They wanted to bless others, and in turn, money seemed to come looking for them and track them down, overtaking them with material and spiritual blessings that they couldn't put a price tag on. Each time a ministry, church or individual would say, "We have enough money, for God is our source," angels would be released to bring in above and beyond what they were believing God for.

Twenty-One

HIT BY A WILD PITCH

Here comes the pitch!... It turns wild as it comes at the batter like a deranged missile. He's unable to back away fast enough, and the ball drills him in the back. All eyes in the stadium, including mine, are immediately riveted on the pitcher, questioning his intentions.

As the batter shakes off the pain, there's something he doesn't do that makes him a star in the game: He doesn't look back at the pitcher who wounded him! Instead, he proudly trots down to first base. Silently his character spoke so loudly that it filled the stadium with reverence and seemed to say, "Thank you, Mr. Pitcher, you didn't strike me out. I still made it to first base!"

At that moment, I felt the Holy Spirit come into that stadium and speak to me. He said, "Bill, how many of My people have been hit by a wild pitch and cannot take their eyes off the pitcher who hurt them and they never get on base because of the hurt?"

I sense that many in the Body of Christ —because of "hits and hurts" —cannot discern who is winning or losing. And they don't know what inning we're in.

I believe many have been up to bat spiritually and have been hit by some wild pitches. Many can't take their eyes off the one who hurt or wounded them. I believe so many in the Body of Christ have gotten hit by wild pitches that we've got all the bases loaded. The good news is we are still up at bat! The bad news is many are afraid of being in the batter's box because they've been hit in the past.

But God is saying, "PICK UP THE BAT OF PRAYER and get back in the batter's box one more time. Pray for those who have hit you with a wild pitch. Pray for those who keep striking you out. Pray for those who throw so many wild pitches at you that you have to end up taking a walk."

There is more than one way to get on base. You can hit the ball. You can get a walk. Or you can get hit by a pitch. Getting hit still gets you on base. I believe God is still in our bat, and I feel a home-run anointing coming over us as the Body of Christ is coming together as an unbeatable team.

I see us hitting the ball so hard that it will go over every wall, hitting the nations, smashing the 10/40 window and every other window to pieces! I see this ball going like a ball inside a pinball machine. Anything it hits only knocks it farther on, hitting strategic landmarks of the enemy across the face of the earth. Every time it hits something, something hits it again and it keeps traveling.

I believe what I'm seeing is the last-day spiritual world series coming upon the earth. The world is about to witness a grand slam from a team they thought would never win, and *you* are next up to bat.

Step inside the batter's box now!

I'm picking up *my* bat.

Twenty-Two

A Spiritual Sonogram of a Very Pregnant Church

I saw in the Spirit a spiritual sonogram of a pregnant church. When there's a pregnancy, you can take a sonogram to see how the pregnancy is coming along. As I was watching this pregnancy come into its final stages, complications were developing. There was great pressure with extended labor pains and frustration in many churches.

A sonogram will show how many babies you are going to have.

The reason many churches are having a difficult time giving birth to what God wants to bring forth is that THERE ARE TWO IN THE WOMB! The reason they feel so restricted is that a double birth is about to take place—AN UNEXPECTED DOUBLE ANSWER TO PRAYER FOR A CHILD.

I sense in the Spirit that many churches have been praying and crying out for a great harvest and unknowingly have conceived in their spiritual wombs more than one seed for more than one birth to advance God's Kingdom.

I sense that now is a time of double portions or blessings—giving birth to twins —for many churches.

Many leaders may fail to see God's bigger picture. There may be double births taking place in one church. Some will think it's the enemy trying to divide their vision of reaching the harvest, but it's actually God's multiplication system being punched in to bless churches with more of His greater vision to reach the lost by birthing more than one vision in a church.

"There is a Kingdom that scatters and yet increases." Sometimes two churches come from one. Don't be surprised to see the Lord birth two churches out of one in some congregations. This may appear on the surface as division or a "church split." Some may even feel like they are being pushed out of a church through unpleasant and complicated circumstances. However, this is a normal part of the divine birthing process, for some would never leave the womb without God's ways and means committee. Many times this is God's way of planting churches to fulfill His plans more effectively.

Many of God's people see a church as rejecting them and pushing them out, instead of realizing that that church is actually giving them birth. It's important to realize that the church you came out of was your spiritual mother who birthed you. "Honor her all the days of your life."

Some spiritual fathers who have founded churches and later watched many in their congregations seemingly desert them fail to see from God's perspective.

These spiritual fathers have actually been used to mature their flock enough for them to leave the nest to fulfill their call in a different place.

> *As you do not know the path of the wind, or how the body is formed in a mother's womb, so you cannot understand the work of God, the Maker of all things. Sow your seed in the morning, and at evening let not your hands be idle, for you do not know which will succeed, whether this or that, or whether both will do equally well.*
>
> Ecclesiastes 11:5-6, NIV

It's interesting that verse five (above) talks about the womb and pregnancy and verse six talks about the sowing of seed for a harvest. These seem to go together in God's Kingdom.

Some churches may have TWIN PURPOSES inside of them—similar purposes, yet different enough that there is the need and the necessity for a godly separation to let them both live. In the natural, twins are looked upon as a blessing, although we know they will need TLC—tender loving care. In the spiritual realm, as in the natural, it is not wrong to have twins but rather a blessing.

Twenty-Three

A BASIN OF WATER AND A TOWEL

In the Spirit, I saw God's foot step down into cities and regions of the earth. I knew that His foot represented great authority coming to earth.

When I saw His foot, I knew He had come to take back territory that the enemy had stolen from His Kingdom. As I began rejoicing at why His foot stepped down upon the earth, He interrupted my praise service with a strong command..."Wash My feet!" I was dumbfounded. I said, "Lord, how could I ever wash Your feet?"

The Lord spoke to me, "When you see pastors and leaders coming together and washing one another's feet, you will see My foot come down with great power releasing whole regions and territories back into My Kingdom. "

I then saw a vision of pastors and leaders humbly kneeling before each other with basins of water and towels. As we began washing one another's feet, titles, positions and even names of churches started drowning in that small basin of water! Pride, jealousy and envy were being drowned in just twelve inches of water! Weary, blistered feet that had lost their way on the dusty, soiled road of life were being healed by just water and the two hands of a pastor from down the street.

Help was never that far away all along.

Tears began filling these basins of water to overflowing…tears of repentance from judging and misunderstanding one another. Even our eyes were being washed with tears to see that we were not each other's enemy but that we were on the same team. It was such a beautiful and humbling sight. Pastors of huge churches and leaders of small churches penitent and bowing before one another confessing our total inability to advance God's Kingdom. Revelation began breaking forth upon us that we needed each other. Many were held in each other's grip breaking together. Holy kisses started being given out upon the faces and the feet. A presence came as though we had kissed the face of God!

At that moment, I saw divine authority flow from the feet of One who was also in our midst. A divine authority and power was being unleashed upon regions and territories. We were shaking the very gates of hell with a basin of water and a towel! It seemed the smaller we became in one another's sight, the bigger God became in the sight of the enemy! God began exalting Himself in the earth and among the heathen.

I heard the Lord speak to the angels who were present during foot washing. He said, "Take the tears from those basins and put them in bottles. They will bring forth a great move of My Spirit to bring in the harvest."

Twenty-Four

A Season of Scattering Seed

I heard the Lord say, "There is a Kingdom that scatters and yet increases."

I saw God's people inside of churches as seeds. I then saw His hand reach down and pick up many of these seeds and begin to scatter them far and near into other fields of ministry and harvest.

I sensed it was seed planting time in the Spirit. Much of God's seed was being scattered by winds of adversity allowed by Him to send these seeds to new places to be planted where they would not have gone on their own. The strong winds that blew many seeds outside of the house were also used to push many seeds inside of the house downward into a deeper commitment to Him and to that house.

Pastors became discouraged, for it seemed like it was a season of losing sheep from their folds. But it was actually God's way of scattering His seed, as these winds were blowing inside the house.

Seeds that remained in the house began to judge the seeds that were leaving. Some seeds that were leaving started to judge the seeds that were meant to stay behind. I heard the Lord say, "It is My seed—don't judge it! This is of Me and it is marvelous in My eyes. My Kingdom is bigger than any one church."

Some seeds that had grown roots downward over many years and had become like strong, faithful trees in their churches, giving shade and comfort to many, were actually uprooted by severe winds and carried away to be transplanted by the Spirit elsewhere, even into other churches that had no shade of a strong, mature tree.

Twenty-Five

A SPIRITUAL CAVE-IN

While praying recently, I saw a spiritual cave-in take place in the Body of Christ. I just knew all of a sudden that many of God's people were trapped beneath circumstances that had caved in upon them with overwhelming force. These who were trapped beneath this cave-in were seemingly separated from God.

These ones were absolutely powerless to do anything for themselves but to cry out hoping against hope to be rescued. They were not all in the same cave-in area, but each one was separately in their own entrapment seemingly cut off from the rest of the Body of Christ. Some were on the verge of giving up and despairing of life itself. They could not seem to live, but neither could they die. This cave-in had buried them alive.

I heard the Lord speak concerning these desperate ones: "Tell these people that though they cannot see Me now, I still see them. Though they cannot hear Me now, I still hear them and their cries. Though it seems I have forgotten them and not answered and they don't understand what has happened, I know where they are and the condition they are in and My eyes are upon them this very moment more than any other time in their life."

I then saw the hand of God begin to move very slowly downward towards the cave-ins —so slowly that many could not notice God's hand moving at all. But it was moving…ever so slowly, but ever so surely. It seemed God was saying that this rescue will not be in a sudden, instant moment of divine intervention. However, little by little and gradually as God's almighty hand moves and pushes back the powers of darkness, the rescue will be carried out.

The frustration of many wanting their deliverance or answer now and not seeing God do it when they think He should is causing them to sink down further in unbelief and causing their hearts to harden against the Lord, who is their only way out.

The Lord was saying, "Tell them to harden not their hearts, for My ways are not their ways, nor My timing their timing. They must be still and cease from striving and know that I am God and that I am going to bring them out. Be patient in tribulation, for in patience you shall possess your souls."

God's hand is moving slowly, but it is moving surely…right towards you! Let not your heart be troubled, neither let it be afraid. God's hand is coming not just to move in circumstances and troubles, but to lay hold upon you to touch, to change and to embrace, to bring you up and out with His right hand of righteousness around you.

"You ask, 'Why so long?' I tell you I am never late… seldom early…but always on time. What I do now you do not understand, but you will know later. Trust Me!"

Twenty-Six

"THE SHAKING IS CONFIRMATION"

I heard the Lord say, "I am about to push the launching pad button for many who have been crying out to Me to go higher in their calling—their calling to know Me. Tell My people to buckle their seat belts, for it is T minus 10 and counting."

As God's finger pushed the launching pad button, immediately a great shaking began taking place in these peoples' lives. This tremendous shaking caused many to wonder if there had been a major malfunction on the launching pad, causing their "higher calling" seemingly to be aborted. Many were convinced that this turbulence was from the enemy.

I then heard a voice from Heaven's Mission Control Center: "That was just the ignition switch. Do not fear the shaking. THE SHAKING IS CONFIRMATION THAT I AM LAUNCHING YOU!"

Simultaneously, flames of fire ignited beneath them. The Lord spoke, "It's the fire that will take you higher." The fire of the Spirit began burning up those things that had kept these people on the launching pad and held them back all of their lives. Through this terrible shaking and testing through fire they were coming to know something greater than their calling—the ONE who has called them! The more they knew Him, the higher He took them.

Like Elijah's chariot of fire, they ascended upward, penetrating the very heavenlies—breaking through barriers of international proportion. I saw a mantle of unprecedented evangelism falling to the earth. It seemed to slip right down from the Father's throne room. It was big enough for the whole earth to wrap around itself twice. The glory of the Lord began covering the earth.

Twenty-Seven

"Cancellations Cannot Cancel Your Destination!"

Are you having a rough time getting to where you think God wants you to be? Recently I flew to Vermont to minister. I had two cancellations in flights, two delays and lost luggage. This trip was so bizarre that it couldn't have been the devil—he is not that big. I said, "Lord, what is going on here? What are You trying to communicate to me?"

I sensed the Lord saying, "Many of My people have experienced cancellations in their lives and ministries. Many have had delays and have been put on hold. Many have lost spiritual luggage that had precious things inside. But...cancellations cannot cancel your destination! I am booking you on another flight—nonstop!

"The reason there have been cancellations for many is because the flight they had planned to go on seemed to be the right flight to them but would not have taken them to where I wanted them to go."

Right flight—wrong destination!

"The delays were divinely ordered, for My timing was not yet. Lost luggage having precious things they wanted to take along was not meant to go where I am taking them. I have allowed many people's luggage to disappear. I am now booking many of these people on another flight—nonstop! This flight will make up for lost time, for My Wind is now beneath their wings.

"This flight will take them above the storms of life and they will see My 'Sonshine' again. This flight will take them higher above every stop sign of the enemy. Many of My people will have to get on this flight by faith, for they would not believe if it were told them where I am taking them. Some will only know their destination when I land the plane."

Final boarding call…

Twenty-Eight

"KEEP YOUR HAND TO THE PLOW!"

I saw a vision of a hand gripping a plow, sweating under the burden of labor in the field of ministry. Coming down onto the plowman's field were fluttering birds, great and small, threatening to steal the seed being sown, greatly distracting the plowman plodding along.

There were high winds of adversity prevailing, with thick, dark clouds of oppression overshadowing this huge field. These present conditions on the ground and in the atmosphere seemed to render this labor all in vain. The hand, being weary and now trembling from discouragement, started slipping hopelessly from the plow. For a brief moment, this vision stood motionless as though the heartbeat of the plowman had stopped.

Suddenly, God's voice, like thunder cracking and booming through the black clouds, touching down like lightning, pierced the plowman's heart making it feel as though it was bursting with electrifying power like a jump start....

"KEEP YOUR HAND TO THE PLOW! KEEP YOUR HAND TO THE PLOW!

"Look not to the right or to the left.

"Don't look back.

"Don't even look ahead.

"But look up and fix your eyes on Me, the Author and Finisher of your labor, for your redemption draweth nigh. Waste no time shooing the birds from your field, but keep your hand to the plow and keep plowing on in hope.

"Know that your labor is not in vain in the Lord and be not weary in well doing, for you shall reap bountifully if you faint not. I am coming into your field of labor to redeem it and to release a new anointing and unction that will break forth upon your ground, for the earth is Mine.

"I am also coming into your ministry, and you will discover power coming upon your plow and going before you, making the crooked places straight and cutting the bars asunder, opening up even new ground and opportunities.

"My strength will come flowing through the plow into your hand, and the blood, sweat and tears sown in discouragement will be reaping in My joy that will become your strength in this last-day harvest. You will discover My strength being made perfect in your weakness and find My joy in your journey.

"For joy is not only found in the reaping, but there will be plenty in the sowing, so much that the days will come, as in Amos 9:13, that *'the plowman shall overtake the reaper,'* says the Lord.

"Remember… *'he that observeth the wind shall not*

sow; and he that regardeth the clouds shall not reap. As thou knowest not what is the way of the spirit,...even so thou knowest not the works of God who maketh all. In the morning sow thy seed, and in the evening withhold not thine hand: for thou knowest not whether shall prosper, either this or that, or whether they both shall be alike good.' (Ecclesiastes 11:4-6).

"KEEP YOUR HAND TO THE PLOW!"

Twenty-Nine

FIERY FURNACE AND LIONS' DEN JUST AHEAD

In the Spirit, I sensed the Lord saying, "I am going to catapult many of My people this hour into strategic positions to accomplish exploits that will cause the world to take note that they have been with My Son, Jesus, who is the way, the truth and the life, whose name is the only name under Heaven whereby men must be saved.

"I am about to honor many and release them, giving them favor with God and man. Men in high places of earthly authority will soon know that there is a God in Heaven who steps down to intermingle with the affairs of men upon the earth by revealing secrets to His servants. These servants will be modern-day Shadrachs, Meshachs, Abednegos and Deborahs, having an excellent spirit, divine wisdom and boldness to speak the word of the Lord with no fear of man."

I then saw a yellow light blinking in the Spirit: "Caution: Fiery Furnace Just Ahead!"

I thought at first this sign was of the enemy to put fear into the Body of Christ as we were pressing forward to know our God and His power in our lives. Surprisingly to me, I heard the voice of our heavenly Father commanding His angels: "Turn up the furnace and make it seven times hotter! I will bring them through the fire. My holy fire changes things that nothing else can. I will burn up those things that hold My people earthbound to the things of this world. The world will see the 'fourth man in the furnace' one more time, and I will deliver My people forever from the fear of fiery furnaces."

Another sign that I saw in the Spirit for the Body of Christ was: "Lions' Den Ahead!" Some coming up for promotion in God's Kingdom seemed to be headed straight towards the mouths of lions. I saw some people turn back at this point as they were shaken by the size of the lions' teeth. Others continued walking right towards what appeared to be certain death. As they proclaimed, "For me to live is Christ and to die is gain" and "Though He slay me, yet will I trust Him," their faith in God paralyzed the enemy and it shut the mouths of these lions.

I sensed the Lord saying, "Tell My people that in their testing and trials they are being watched by a great cloud of witnesses from on high." I saw loved ones who had gone on before us standing in the grandstands of Glory cheering and shouting: "Keep going! Don't stop now! Your God is bringing you through!"

And then the Lord said, "The world will be watching their responses during their testings to see if they are going to walk their talk. And forever My eyes will be upon them and I will be monitoring their situations and tests. Tell My people whatever difficulties they are going through, the good news is they are going through! This is only a test to bring forth a testimony. And I will take their mess to bring forth a message this hour that will touch many who will see and hear what I can do."

These believers coming up for promotion in the Kingdom of God were people who were willing to say, "Our God is able to deliver us, but if He chooses not to, we will still trust in Him."

Thirty

"Come Out of the Cave"

While in Israel, I hiked to the cliffs of En Gedi. The mountain cliffs of En Gedi were where David hid in caves from King Saul. David was anointed to be the next king over Israel, but he went into hiding because of his pursuing enemy. You can have a great call of God and destiny on your life but still be in hiding.

The Lord spoke to me up near those caves where David hid. God said, "Tell My people to come out of their caves. Their Sauls have been slain. Your enemies have been slain. Come out of your caves of fear, caves of doubt, caves of unbelief. Come out—I want to use you! This day the spirit of Saul that has hounded you and has driven you into caves, intimidating you, is being destroyed."

There is a cave in En Gedi that can hold three thousand soldiers. Whole churches can be in a cave, intimidated by the enemy.

In the Spirit, I saw some caves that you may have difficulty coming out of to go forward into God's purposes for your life. The biggest cave I saw in the Spirit was called "The Fear of the Lack of Finances" to accomplish what God is calling you to do.

A revelation jumped into my spirit of what is written on our money: on our currency and on every coin. It says: "In God We Trust." God spoke to me: "Tell My people, 'Don't count your money—read it! Don't count how much you have or don't have; count Me.... Count Me into your God-given destiny.'"

We are not to be led by money, but we are to be led by His Spirit. We must find out what God wants us to do and then trust Him and step out of that cave.

Another cave I saw was "The Fear of the Unknown." What's out there? I don't know; let's go find out! Many want to wait and know all the details before stepping out of the cave. But God doesn't tell us everything at once. Revelation follows obedience. God speaks as He confirms what *He* wants us to do. Then obedience must follow. Then He explains...maybe. Abraham went out not knowing where he was going, and he ended up with a city whose builder and maker was God.

Another cave was "A More Convenient Time," but there will never be a convenient time for our flesh to feel like stepping out for God. *"Now faith is"* (Hebrews 11:1).... Faith is for now.

Another cave was called "My Plans." Someone once said, "If you want to hear God laugh, tell Him your plans, and if you want to laugh, wait 'til you hear His!" We must leave our plans in the cave as we step out into His purposes.

There was a cave called "The Fear of Failing." What

if we fail as we step out? Listen…what if we don't? It's in the fall that we learn to fly. God is stirring our nest of comfort like a mother eagle to get us out on the edge of the nest so He can give us a love push over the edge, for we were not born to stay in the nest but to learn like the eaglet that it is through falling that we learn to flap our wings and fly with the wind that's beneath us.

One of the largest caves I saw was "The Cave of Past Failure." This cave held us back from the present and the future. When I was on the Sea of Galilee about halfway across, I said to the Lord, "Lord, this is the sea where You called Peter out of the boat and Peter walked on the water before he fell in." I said, "Lord, are we near the place where Peter got out of the boat and walked on water before he fell?"

The Lord answered me, "What do you mean Peter fell? This is the sea where Peter walked!" as though He didn't understand my question. Listen…He doesn't see your failure either. If you have confessed your sins and failures to Him, they are gone, gone, gone. They are not even on the bottom of the Sea of Forgetfulness. The fish ate them! God did not see the last time you fell. He only saw the last time you got back up! Come out of "The Cave of Past Failure." God has need of you.

By faith, I am going to blow the shofar into your caves and you are going to come out…ready or not! The breath of God is going to blow you out of every cave of hiding, and His breath will blow every cave in, so you will not be able to go back into them. Even the dust from those caves falling in will praise Him.

The Lord says to you, "Come out with your hands up. Leave everything in the cave. You won't need it." He has new things to give you to fulfill His purposes. Right now His breath is blowing. Step out now. God has need of you. This is your last "cave day." Receive His breath and be blown into your destiny.

Thirty-One

A RECALL ON MINISTERS WHO HAVE QUIT THE MINISTRY

Like a news bulletin out of Heaven, I heard the Lord giving a recall on ministers who have quit the ministry mainly because of discouragement. I heard the Lord announcing to thousands of ministers who have given up on their ministries and walk with Him: "I never call you to quit by using discouragement. Discouragement is from the enemy, and it only confirms that I have a greater calling on you than you realize. My gifts and calling are without repentance. My calling is still on you, and I am calling you back to Me with a fresh anointing to serve Me.

"With love, I am giving you space to return to the path I had laid out for you. This opportunity comes complete with My gifts and anointing. If you simply repent and humble yourselves before Me and others, I will open up the door that closed behind you when you left. Also, many of you will find that new and different doors will now open up for you, for I was in the process of adjusting your gifts and callings when the enemy convinced you to give up and leave where you were. I had plans to move many of you to a new place of ministry if you would have waited just a little longer for Me to move people around you. But even now it is not too late, for I am giving you a window of opportunity to say yes again to Me, to allow Me to finish the work I have planned for you to do.

"An even greater anointing awaits you, for I will use you to recall the backsliders, prodigals and many of My people who have given up on the inside though they still appear content going through the motions and seem to be doing great works for Me.

"You are needed in My harvest field more than ever. If you will overcome the lies of the enemy and others telling you that you are a failure, you will begin to see what I can do with what they think a failure is. I will show the world I have no failures. Your temporary pit stop in the race set before you will prove to be a recharging and refueling experience as I call you back onto the course of your destiny. I will use it to launch you toward the finish line with My power sending you!

"Remember Joseph's dream started in a pit and ended in a palace!

"I am calling all ministers who thought they'd quit and that I was through with them. But I am now recalling them.

"Can you hear Me now?"

Thirty-Two

"SWING THE PENDULUM!"

In the Spirit, I saw the angels obeying a heavenly command, pushing a huge pendulum in the opposite direction than it had previously swung, which was so far into that degradation of sin and wickedness that it appeared to be unstoppable.

I then heard the Father say, "It's time to call forth the noble, the wealthy and the renowned of the earth. I'm going to turn the world upside down, inside out and right side up!"

I then saw the spirit of integrity begin to descend upon dignitaries, celebrities and the very elite.

In the Spirit, I sensed the Lord saying, "There is a certain caliber of society that has been overlooked and given up hope for by many of My people, who have even stopped praying for them. But again it will be proven that it is by My Spirit, and My Spirit is being poured out upon *all* flesh."

I saw very influential people being drawn by God's Spirit into His Kingdom. I saw dignitaries, celebrities and the very elite being drawn into the House of the

Lord. I saw some of them coming to church in armored cars with security guards around them...but they were coming! I saw, at times, helicopters landing in church parking lots, bringing in dignitaries from high positions of government. Some were walking through the front doors of churches with bodyguards because of their honor and prestige. The high and mighty as well as the lowly were coming into the Father's House now.

Integrity was gripping their hearts to hunger for and honor the King who, they were realizing, had given them power, wealth and high positions in the land. I saw one very prominent person, whose name was known throughout the nations, put a check in the offering plate in one service that was large enough to meet the church budget for the next five years! The tithe from this one check went out from this church to support all their missionaries for a full year!

These dignitaries and wealthy ones who had been filled with God's integrity and glory could rarely stay in one church for very long, because of the publicity, and because they were making some religious people uncomfortable. As a result, the Holy Spirit would lead them to different churches, to visit and receive counsel and wisdom from many different styles of worship, and revelatory teaching from more than just one minister, thereby receiving the whole counsel of God.

Cross-pollination was vital for them, as they would visit different churches to receive various revelations to help lead a nation. In the meantime, many churches were being blessed, experiencing the presence of integrity brought by these elite visitors from a caliber of society where integrity is rarely found. This presence was a result of the dignitary's service to the Lord in places where integrity was absent.

I heard the King of kings say: "When you begin to see the kings of the earth and high government officials and the upper class being drawn into My House, honor these kings and their high positions and know that the time is soon when the King of kings and Lord of lords will appear in all of His glory in His House. Get used to honoring those in high places and those who are gifted with talent that astounds the world. Continue to pray, believing for their souls.

"I have said that 'not many mighty and not many noble are called.' I didn't say 'not any.' I said 'not many.' I have said, 'It is easier for a camel to go through the eye of a needle than for a rich man to enter into the Kingdom of Heaven,' but I didn't say it was impossible for him to enter."

The pendulum is beginning to swing. Now it will touch not only the poor and lowly, but also the rich, the famous and those in high places.

I heard God say, "All rise…. The kings, queens, princes and rulers of nations are coming in on this next move.

"Swing that pendulum!"

Thirty-Three

ANGELS PLANTING SEEDS IN GROUND ZERO

As men were still digging and clearing away the debris at Ground Zero, in New York City, I saw angels standing guard around this piece of property as though it will be used for future divine purposes. There were bags of seeds these angels had brought on the scene waiting for the ground to be dug a little deeper. They appeared to be "seed-planting angels"— angels who specialized in planting spiritual seeds into places on the earth where the enemy had wreaked horrific destruction on mankind.

One strong angel had the word "Redeem" written all over him. He appeared anxiously excited to start sowing this ground with seeds of life. The bags of seeds around this angel had powerful prophetic words from Heaven written all over them:

"O thou afflicted, tossed with tempest, and not comforted, behold, I will lay thy stones with fair colors, and lay thy foundations with sapphires."
Isaiah 54:11

"Behold, thy salvation cometh.... and thou shalt be called, Sought out, A city not forsaken."
Isaiah 62:11-12

"I will redeem you."   Exodus 6: 6

Another strong angel had countless larger bags of bottled tears. There were rivers of tears the Lord had collected and put into bottles: tears from those who lost loved ones, even the tears that were shed by many who were crying out to God in their dying moments.

I now have an assurance that the mercy of God allowed many to have that moment to cry out to Him. In the Spirit, I heard many crying out to Jesus in their dying moments because of seeds planted in their lives long before.

All these tears were now about to be poured upon Ground Zero. It looked like a flood of tears was about to be released to water these seeds. I heard an angel proclaiming, "When the enemy comes in, like a flood the Spirit of the Lord will raise up a standard against him!"

It dawned on me what that standard was and will continue to be in the future to redeem us and our nation. God's standard is tears! Ongoing tears from us crying out to Him will be as vital as the tears of the ones who cried out to Him with their last breath—and as real as the crying of the ones who lost loved ones and who have cried out all their tears.

I sense the Lord proclaiming, "Call for the weeping women to travail before Me. Call for the men who have never shed tears. Call for the children to cry out to Me. Ongoing tears will be needed for a future harvest. Tears will be the spiritual fertilizer to water and nourish My Word being planted into Ground Zero in New York and in the ground zeros in your own personal lives and families."

I heard the Lord whisper, "When you are at your ground zero, there's Me."

Thirty-Four

THE HEARTS OF THE LOST ARE OPENING UP

In the Spirit, I saw an unprecedented move of God like never before begin to sweep over multitudes that were lost. I saw the doors of their hearts opening up from the inside out and then beginning to fall off as their hinges were being melted by the love of God. What was happening that finally was changing these hearts of stone to hearts of flesh?

It was like a video was rewinding and I saw a huge angel flashing a sword downward from the heavenlies over the Body of Christ as we were crying out with fasting for the lost. I then saw this sword sever the jugular vein of a Goliath lying spirit that had deceived many of God's people, telling them: "Don't share Jesus with your neighbors! They are not really open and you will only turn them off more!" This lying spirit had paralyzed many from reaching out to the lost and held them inside their prayer closets and solemn assemblies crying out to God to bring in the lost Himself.

As this lying spirit like a stronghold began to fall,

the Body of Christ began to believe the opposite was true. Even as the Gospel was hidden from the lost by a veil of blindness over them, we began to realize that the lost had been hidden even from us. For we had closed our eyes to pray for them for so long that we had failed to really see them.

I then heard the Father in Heaven saying to a strong angel, "Tell them to pray for the lost with eyes wide open or they will miss opportunities that are coming right in front of them! The lost have been ready. My people just didn't believe it! The lost are so ripe for the harvest that you won't even need to carry your Bible. Let my Word now be flesh in you. Your hands must be free to embrace them, for just a hug of love will cause many in this harvest to literally fall head-long into My Kingdom as I reach out through you. Even let your words be few and just listen as they pour out their hearts, for they are dying to be accepted and loved as I have loved you. Just be there for them."

I saw something like an automatic door that opens when you walk close to it. When you get so close, the door automatically opens without you pushing it or even touching it. You don't even have to ask the door if it would like to open up for you—it just does.

I saw in the Spirit this same principle between the Body of Christ and the lost as we would just begin to walk and come near them. The doors of their hearts would just begin to open up to us and allow us into their lives as though they had been waiting for us to come to them for a long time. I sensed the secret of what was opening their hearts now was the un-threatening, loving way we came toward them. It was like all we had was the love of

God flowing through us and upon them, and they just simply started giving away their hearts and lives to the Lord totally.

I then heard the Lord whisper to us, flooding our hearts with His compassion as we began to perceive the harvest all around us. He was bringing it to where we were. It was like we didn't even have to go, because it had now come to us so ripe and ready. The Lord whispered, "Walk softly, for the harvest now is at your feet. It's that close. And they are ready and waiting for you."

Thirty-Five

A HIDDEN GUN IN THE CASKET

In the Spirit, I saw many in the Body of Christ seemingly lying in a casket that was closing upon them. As the casket lid was closed and their final breath was being taken, their trembling hand felt something inside that closed coffin of death! Lying right on the inside of the lining of the casket their hand felt the outline of what seemed to be a handgun engraved with heavenly writing: "PERSEVERING PRAYER." On the trigger of this gun was etched in minute, almost invisible letters: "WE NEVER GIVE UP!"

The trembling hand with one last persevering prayer laid hold of the handgun and then by blind faith in the midst of total darkness aimed towards the hinges of the casket. The next split second I saw the hinges of caskets being blown away from the inside out all across the earth and many escaping premature death.

I then heard a strong angel declaring from the heavenlies: "They found it! They found it! They found the key to the miraculous! They didn't quit but persevered in intercession in the face of death against terminal diseases, sickness and infirmities, beating all the odds!"

I then heard another angel in Heaven proclaim: "Tip the bowl over!" I then saw a bowl of prayers from earth that had risen up and filled a huge bowl in Heaven over a period of many long years. Written on the side of this huge bowl were the words "THE REPORT OF THE LORD." The bowl was tipped over, and out poured signs, wonders and miracles upon the earth. Prayers that seemingly didn't get answered in the past were not prayed in vain. These same prayers were rising up and being counted and were filling this huge bowl of intercession in Heaven that was now being poured out to bring a mighty move of healing and resurrection power upon the earth.

Not only was there healing, with divine health replacing sickness, but I heard a strong angel decreeing throughout the earth, "Cancel those funerals! Their time is not yet. I am giving them the key to unlock the jaws of death and release resurrection life. With long life will I satisfy them and show them My salvation."

In closing, I heard the Father command, "Pull the trigger again!"

Thirty-Six

EXCHANGING NAMES FOR CHRISTMAS

In the Spirit, I saw churches exchanging one another's names for Christmas and the New Year just like many families do this time of year in order to show their love to each other through exchanging gifts.

I heard the Lord speaking to many pastors and churches this season: "Would you be willing to take the name of a church near you (any church as long as it is not yours) and pray that I will bless it with spiritual fruit baskets and My gifts of the Spirit and bring a mighty move of Me upon it?"

This Father's request seemed so untimely to many, for most pastors and churches were already overwhelmed with their own problems and trials. It seemed they needed more prayer themselves, for they were not experiencing honest breakthroughs in their own churches.

But a few desperate pastors and churches were so hungry for a move of God anywhere—even in the church down the street if need be—that they began to pray outside of the desires and needs of themselves and their own churches.

I saw the enemy tremble as churches were taking their eyes and minds off their own selves and thinking of others by praying for the church next door. The enemy started screaming to his demons, "Don't let them forget about themselves and their own problems, for that alone will become half of their victory! The other half of victory for them will be if they even think about blessing that church next door—that thing we dread the most—the habitation of God—will cancel our assignment to write 'Ichabod' over their own front door!"

A powerful exchange was happening. Not only were names of churches being exchanged in the Spirit, but as these churches began to pray for one another, their strengths were being exchanged also with each other and were canceling out one another's weaknesses.

Each church seemed to have a certain strong anointing and gift that began to be exchanged with each other as they prayed. I heard the Lord decreeing over these churches: "Confess your faults one to another, and pray one for another, that you may be healed."

As churches continued praying one for another, "gifts" from hell that had been postmarked and delivered to their front doors began to be nullified as angels encamped around these churches began to stamp these assignments "UNDELIVERABLE: RETURN TO SENDER."

I saw snow falling in the Spirit upon these churches.

Love was covering and a cleansing from sin was taking place as a pure "presence" of the Lord became the greatest "present" we were receiving together. It was beginning to look a lot like Christmas!

This exchanging of names by the Holy Spirit seemed not only for the Christmas season, but for the whole New Year!

As the birth of Christ was being celebrated this season through these churches praying for each other, I sensed that new spiritual births, multiple births of miracles and the power of healings would take place in these churches in the coming year as they continued praying one for another.

Thirty-Seven

RAMS' HORNS AND DANCING FEET OVER WASHINGTON, D.C.

In the Spirit, I saw the initials of the District of Columbia—D.C.— lighting up, standing for "Divine Combat." The weapons God will use to help take this city will not be carnal, but mighty through Him to the pulling down of strongholds.

Then I heard the Lord say, "The army I'm raising up will be few in number, and their weapons will appear foolish to many. But My foolishness is wiser than man, and My strategic plans will be hidden from the enemy by My glory as I maneuver My army by My Spirit."

I saw two of the most powerful weapons being called to this city for major breakthroughs: rams' horns and dancing feet! Then the Lord said, "As in Gideon's army, shofars will be blown, breaking many hindrances to release the light of My glory, as though erecting a lighthouse on the front lawn of the White House."

I saw seeds of truth being pushed and planted into

the ground by dancing feet. I saw their roots going down deep and their fruit coming upward, cracking the marble floor inside the White House, cracking the very foundation of deception and greed...exposing the enemy. (The enemy is not a man, but Satan.)

Again the Lord spoke to me: "Though this army is few in number, compared to over a million men I drew to D.C. (Promise Keepers' Stand in the Gap event), do not be discouraged. Your assignment is different. Though they are few in number, I am going to amplify the sound of My weapons. Their sound will be heard inside the White House by enemy strongholds. I will amplify it to the degree that it will sound to the enemy like a million shofars and a million dancing feet have come to town! The echo will carry across the nation."

Recently I saw again the initials of the city of Washington, D.C., lighting up as another powerful weapon. This time the initials D.C. were standing for "Dear Children." Children will be used to help take the city.

Thirty-Eight

"I WILL BEGIN TO REDEEM THE MEDIA IN 2004"

I sense that there's something in the air. It's as though Heaven is descending a little closer to earth. The prince of the power of the air is being divinely interfered with and massively interrupted.

I heard Heaven proclaim: "The time has come to redeem the airwaves covering the earth and to begin to impact the media to become a conduit to pour out My Spirit upon all flesh."

I then saw angels beginning to anoint satellite stations and dishes above the earth. And on the earth, angels were descending upon huge television and radio towers. Great heavenly broadcasting interference was about to come upon the earth.

Angels were being assigned to billboards, newspapers and nationwide magazines. Even addresses of pornographic empires were being given to angels for assignments.

Anything the angels could get their hands on was about to be used to alert people to the great outpouring of God's love and judgment coming to earth. Computer online services would feel the weight of God's glory impacting them.

Divine favor was being given to many ministries with the media beginning in the year 2004 to go nationwide and worldwide. A hunger for the supernatural and the miraculous caused television and radio talk shows to open up for testimonies of genuine healings and heavenly visitations that would be broadcast around the world. News reporters were beginning to lean towards unusual stories of awesome happenings that were leaving their listeners with the idea "There must be a God in Heaven!"

In closing, I sense the Father saying: "I will use even the air itself to testify of My power and might. From shore to shore in 2004…I will begin to become the desire of the nations!"

Contact the Author

Blowing the Shofar Ministries
Bill Yount
132 East North Ave.
Hagerstown, MD 21740

blowtheshofar@juno.com

www.billyount.com